IDENTITY BRANDING

"Written by a Pro, for the 'Pro' – a must read…offerir
that can be put to immediate use."
Matt Oechsli, The Oechsli Institute, /

"Creative and distinctive ideas…Strategies that are pruven winners for the financial services
professional. Cannot help but make you a success!"
Bill Brooks, The Brooks Group, Author of High Impact Selling

"Dizzy Dean said, 'It ain't braggin' if you've done it. Krumroy not only knows what he's talking
about, but he's done it!"
Ron Willingham, Integrity Systems, Inc., Author of Integrity Selling

"A marketing pioneer has given us a road map for the future. A must read for any financial
professional wanting to survive."
Wallace F. Dale, Database Equity, Inc., Author of Collaborative Database Marketing

" 'Leading edge' ideas on marketing and positioning…should be required reading."
Dennis R. Merideth, CLU, ChFC,
President of the National Association of Insurance and Financial Advisors, 2000-2001

"Best I've ever read…should be a must for any practitioner."
William D. Pollakov, President-Elect of the General Agents and Managers Association, 2001

"Insightful and impressive…presented to those that are determined to excel, not just survive."
Allan G. Hancock, CLU, ChFC, Past President of the National Association of Life Underwriters,
past delegate to the White House Conference on Small Business

"For the financial professional seeking long term, meaningful marketplace validation. Ignore his
message at your own peril!"
Paul F. Donohue, CRMS, President of MoneyNet

"If you want the 'how to' for becoming known in your market place; becoming an effective CEO
of your financial services business…read and digest these insights."
Jack and Garry Kinder, Kinder Brothers International

"Concepts and vision for 'Branding' – accurate, thought provoking, intriguing – goes beyond the
basic Madison Avenue drivel. In this new age of competitive warfare and change, this book will
show you how to thrive. A must read."
Guy Baker, CLU, MSFS, Top of the Table
Author of Why People Buy, MDRT Foundation President, 2000

"Written for those who want to thrive, a must read…solid advice, examples to model, up-to-the-
minute resources…you can gain an almost unfair advantage!"
Pamela Yellen, CEO, Prospecting & Marketing Institute, Inc.

"This book is superb. Someone has finally defined the "illusion" of marketing with logic and clarity.
The breadth of EXAMPLES and practical guidelines are priceless…immediately useful for
becoming DISTINCT and differentiated in today's competitive marketplace! This is a masterpiece
that will redefine the training and focus for sales professionals within the financial services
industry."
Charles A. Smith, CLU, ChFC, Executive Vice President and
CEO of the General Agents and Managers Association (GAMA) International

IDENTITY BRANDING

© Robert E. Krumroy, 2000

Given the current legal environment, we suggest that you consult your compliance or legal advisors before adapting the ideas presented in this book. We have not intentionally included any advice or materials that put you at risk, but we also realize how quickly and often laws and regulations change regarding the financial services industry.

This publication is designed to provide accurate and authoritative information in regard to the subject matter covered. It is sold with the understanding that neither the author or the publisher is engaged in rendering legal, accounting, or other professional service. If legal advice or other expert assistance is required, the services of a competent professional person should be sought.

From a Declaration of Principles jointly adopted by a committee of the American Bar Association and a Committee of Publishers.

Michelle J. Polczynski, Design Consultant

Lifestyles Press, Greensboro, NC
ISBN: 0-9678661-0-3

Dedication

Dedicated to the financial sales professional, whose long-term success and personal career satisfaction has been built on a foundation of *"giving"* and not *"getting."* Whose focus of giving value and enhancing the lives of those they touch has been extended not only to their clients but, also, to their entire community. This professional's commitment to *"giving"* has established them as the *Identity Brand* within their local market and has rewarded them with continuous access to prospect communities that welcome their presence. It is this sales professional that stands as a role model to emulate, and the subject matter to which this book is dedicated.

Thank you.

IDENTITY BRANDING

distinct or extinct

"Creating Prospect Attraction"

by **Robert E. Krumroy**

TABLE OF CONTENTS

Section 1: The Critical Issues

Section 2: How Did We Get Here?

Section 3: Networking, Finding Prospects and Capturing "Mindshare"

Section 4: How to Get Started

Section 5: Keeping on Track

FOREWORD

The change that Henry Ford caused by revolutionizing industry through mass production is soon going to be rivaled only by the change that consumers are going to have on how products are purchased and distributed in America. The financial service industry's two primary components for its past success has been focused on developing competitive products and then training or contracting an existing sales force to sell them to the public. In the past, if company revenues began to flatten, products were reviewed to make sure that they were still competitive. If the products proved to be satisfactory, sales systems and sales management were reviewed to discover where the problem was in distribution. Emphasizing quality product features and benefits in conjunction with possessing a proficiency in selling and prospecting skills were the two primary components believed to be necessary for conducting a successful sales encounter. In other words, develop a quality product and find a sales person to deliver it to the customer. I wish sales were still that simple...NO MORE!

The consumer is redefining our formula for success. There is a new discernment that the consumer is applying in making a purchasing decision. That discernment is not predicated on your proficiency in selling or prospecting, but on your proficiency in marketing. Marketing is no longer a skill-module to be mastered after you have been in sales for a period of time. Marketing will become your new business foundation, the universe around which every other system rotates, if you expect to be successful in the future.

Ultimately, this book is about YOU. It's about creating an Identity Brand that attracts customers, increases market access, improves your profits and builds prospect and client loyalty. It is about building a prospect highway to a prospect community and then branding your distinct, unique, intriguing and differentiated identity into their minds, which creates a competitive advantage and welcomes your contact. It's what you do to get the customer to notice you *FIRST.* It's about providing a clear answer to the prospect's question, "Why you?," before ever having a face-to-face encounter.

Before you read this book, I encourage you to answer the following ten questions and then to ponder the answers, some of which may surprise and challenge your current beliefs, but all of which are based on the material in this book. The chapters, thereafter, will provide marketing examples, ways for you to capture "mindshare," practical guidelines for creating market distinction and prospect preference - skills which you must master in the new and very exciting future. The journey is just beginning. Let's get started.

The Ten Question Marketing Checkup

1) Do you believe that focusing *training to specific areas* such as financial planning, financial profiles, the small business market or long-term care for the over age fifty-five population is marketing?

2) Have you identified a market segment(s) in which you are systematically gathering individual names of prospects (individualized marketing), or have you proclaimed a general market segment *in name only,* such as the small business market, as your focus?

3) When was the last time you or your manager(s) allocated a significant block of *structured time* to discuss marketing strategies to a specific market segment? Is this repeated quarterly? Yearly? Every so often?

4) Do you believe that creating a *Web site* is part of the answer for meeting the new marketing challenges of the consumer?

5) How does your organization *define marketing?*

   A) Identifying markets?

   B) Increasing selling skills?

   C) Product development?

   D) Corporate advertising?

   E) Building relationships?

6) Do you believe that providing *great service* enhances marketing?

7) Do you believe that media or print *advertising* can create local market access?

8) Do you believe that utilizing *direct mail* and *telemarketing* are complementary to your marketing efforts?

9) What are the differences between *target selling* and *target marketing?*

10) Do you believe that one of the major objectives for increasing *company name recognition* is to increase sales?

The Ten Question Marketing Answers

1) Training systems and product knowledge, whether advanced or basic, are not components of marketing. Skills and knowledge are very important. If you don't have them, you will find yourself disadvantaged. You will either not be able to deliver what the client expected from your initial encounter or, all things being equal, you will lose the case due to incompetence. You want to be prepared when a selling opportunity exists or when you have an opportunity to talk to a prequalified prospect, but unless you can get into the right doors without having to coerce your way in, you will eventually become the "de-fanged lion", the senior agent with lots of potential but a consistent underachiever. Marketing is about capturing *"mindshare."* It's about building an advantage that opens doors to prospects through creating a *perception* of a *distinct preference* over the competition.

2) There are two major components that need to be mastered in order to be successful in sales. They are (1) *what to say* and (2) to *whom to say it.* However, the second element, "to whom to say it" is probably more misunderstood than any other issue. Most agents think that the first skill is the selling skill, how do I get money from the prospect in return for what I am selling, and the second skill is the prospecting skill, how do I find someone who needs what I have to offer and can afford to pay for it? Sales are just not that simple today.

The proliferation of products in today's society and the broken promises and expectations of performance have led all of us into the age of skepticism. Warranties were created in the mid-1900s as a response to consumer irritation, not as a positive statement about product performance, but because products didn't deliver what the salespeople promised. As product development has progressed and more products appear the same, consumers view most company products as equal. Approaches with promises of better performance, service or competitiveness fall on deaf ears. They are no longer a reason for *"letting you in."*

Market access is the number-one problem that keeps people from succeeding or progressing to new heights. If you can't "get in," your skills of prospecting and selling are useless. In order to "get in," you must become differentiated from the consumer's view of parity among your competitors. You need to create a visible *distinction,* something that is creatively consistent and makes a statement as to who you are, something that attracts the prospect before they have met you. This is called *"capturing mindshare."* It is THE marketing skill.

How do you position yourself to become favorably viewed before you have met? You develop an **Identity Brand, YOU,** and then familiarize the prospect with you through unique experiences in *advance* of your first personal contact. This can only be successfully accomplished if you have successfully identified, on an individual basis, the prospects with whom you would like to do business. These names are valued and never lost. Relationships are cultivated with them over time. They are the people you invite to events and to whom you send newsletters. They are the people who make up your *Prospect Fishbowl*^{TM}. Once they are *individualized,* your primary job shifts from finding prospects to seeking opportunities to migrate within their midst. MIGRATION replaces prospecting as your primary focus.

3) Successful marketing requires two elements. It requires a well thought out plan based on creativity and it requires consistent monitoring as to its progress (we would suggest quarterly). Great marketing is not the result of common sense; it is not working harder nor increasing staff to provide more responsive service; it

is not better activity supervision. Marketing is about building relationships. It is about doing *different* things than the competition, rather than doing the same things in different ways. If the competition is going left, you go right. If they are doing X, you do Y. It is about creating a *distinct uniqueness* that is pleasing to your specific market segment. It is created through innovation, not imitation. It is about capturing the entire market, not market share. It requires the allocation of specific thought time directed toward creating a unique and differentiated plan that is action based.

4) Creating a Web site will not be adequate to meet the communication technology expectations of your clients. Web sites are similar to name recognition programs. *They will not attract prospects.* They may provide a heightened client confidence that you are keeping current, but they do not create initial prospect preference. They will not open doors to new prospects nor give you a marketing advantage.

Communication technology will become an enhancement to building deeper relationships with clients and prospects. In the near future, you will have consumers who expect you to contact them through interactive emails and telecommunication conferencing. They will prefer meeting with you through Internet communication rather than meeting at an arranged location and, if you can't do it, they will find someone who can. They will want newsletters and communications sent via email instead of hard copy. Since many of your current clients prefer that today, imagine the demand in the future. Will you be ready?

Häagen Dazs® Ice Cream currently offers a certificate for one FREE pint of whatever Häagen Dazs product you desire. They request that you fill in your name and email address on the back of the certificate so that they can keep you up to date with "product news, additional coupons and more"...I wonder what "more" means. I wonder what they have in mind. I wonder if they even know. Probably not, but they are smart enough to know that a technology revolution is getting ready to grip America with marketing implications we have never experienced. This ice cream company wants your email address! They know that they are going to communicate differently in the future. What are you doing to *build an email database* that prepares you for the same revolution that even an ice cream company is anticipating?

5) Marketing is the most misunderstood issue in sales today. Most people cannot define the difference between selling and marketing and frequently use the terms interchangeably. The term "market identification" has also been wrongly substituted for marketing, however, it is just a part of prospecting. Consider the owner of a shoe store who identifies the adults in his city who wear size ten shoes, but does not create any distinction that would cause them to buy from him instead of his competition. Marketing is building "mindshare" in prospective customers so that when they need shoes, you are the first person who comes to mind.

Many people think in terms of selling when they think of marketing. You need to have a good selling system, but unless you can gain access to the prospect, you will not be able to apply your selling skills often enough to meet your goals. Additionally, unless the prospect can answer the question, "Why you?," they may not purchase even when you have demonstrated the need and the corresponding solution. "Why you?" is a function of relationship building, not your proficiency, product nor skill.

Many home offices think that **product development** is marketing. After all, they assembled consumer focus groups to get reaction to pre-product development design and then put together the newest product with the best benefits. This may be market-driven product development, but it is not marketing. It will not affect the issue of *"getting in"* to see the prospect. It will not improve agent retention, nor will the newest product take the senior agent who is stalled to a market that better matches his skill level.

Corporate advertising and promotion is the most sensitive issue to address. To some, it is like attacking mother and apple pie. Corporate advertising does serve a purpose. It can help give the agent credibility at the point of sale. It can provide a comfort level to the consumer who recognizes the company by name. It is a significant factor in helping to recruit experienced agents or attracting experienced producers to represent your product. It is helpful in instilling pride in your agents. It is a major factor in the promotion of your stock to the individual investor or the institutional investor and, therefore, helps to maintain a higher stock price. But, corporate advertising does not affect the local agent's ability to "get in," to see the desired prospect.

Marketing is all about **building relationships**. It is about capturing "mindshare." It is about becoming the standard of excellence in a market segment that you will eventually own. It is about becoming Identity Branded as distinct from your competition and unique to a specific market segment that you have individualized.

6) Giving great service is important and it is expected. Always deliver what you promise. If you don't, you will hamper your client retention efforts and ruin your general reputation among your clients. Negative news is passed along ten times the rate and fifty times the impact that positive news is passed along. Service is expected and it is important. Service is what keeps clients but it is not what attracts prospects. *Service is not a marketing issue.*

7) Print or media advertising, even if done in the local market, will not increase accessibility to new prospects. It will not open doors. Print advertising may help increase identification, but it is *brand*

personality that creates consumer pull and prospect attraction. Building preference starts with an experience. Once you have positively influenced the prospect with enough experiences, you develop "mindshare" or as Guy E. Baker, CLU, ChFC says, you get placed on the "shelf of the mind." It is YOU, your personality, your distinction that you build relative to the marketplace and the corresponding emotional connection that influences the consumer. Unfortunately, print advertising is the most frequently thought of item when people think of marketing. It is the easiest so-called "marketing" item to implement, but it is also the *single greatest waste of money* that sales professionals ever spend.

8) The United States currently has only six percent of the world's population yet approximately sixty percent of the world's advertising dollars are spent in this country. The average consumer is exposed to over 3,000 advertising images per day, receives over 1,200 junk mailings per year and is irritated by an average of five telemarketing calls per day. Product proliferation is at an all-time high. People truly do have less time and are more frustrated than in the decades past. All the propaganda and the intrusion marketing methods used to try to sell them are more irritating than at any time in history. Privacy invasion counter measures, from filtering phone calls to getting off of junk-mail lists, is a congressional issue. Direct-mail campaigns and telemarketing programs are not part of the marketing definition. Marketing builds relationships. These methods destroy relationships. Their strategy is based on an antiquated selling model and not on a marketing model.

9) Many agents believe that marketing means telling your story to a group of people instead of to one person at a time. This can, indeed, be part of a marketing strategy. However, just conducting seminars with the idea of selling some of the attendees is not target marketing. *It is target selling.* If seminars are part of your strategy plan of providing continual familiarization to your

Prospect Fishbowl or creating more names for your *Prospect Fishbowl*, it is marketing. To be regarded as marketing, your seminar needs to be focused on building long-term relationships that will lead to preference as well as sales. They need to be one of the elements of a structured marketing plan; developed to create positive experiences for your individualized market segment through consistent familiarity with *the same invited audience.* Doing one-time seminars to create sales will never build the prospect highway to a prospect community that continually welcomes you back.

10) National advertising for companies creates greater name awareness. However, name awareness does not create local market preference, particularly for an intangible, infrequently used product. Nor, will it have an effect on creating easier local market access to the prospect. Name recognition is not what creates consumer attraction, *brand personality* does. Brand personality is built through positive experiences at the local level. These experiences need to be unique, high in value, memorable and differentiated from the market competition. Consumers in the financial services market don't buy a name, nor do they buy based on product. They buy based on *perception.* They buy on what they perceive is a superior *"package of value."* That package of value is based on emotional bonds that you have built through the process of creating continual familiarity with you...the Identity Brand.

IDENTITY BRANDING

The Critical Issues

IDENTITY BRANDING

Innovation – Not Imitation
First – Not Better
Perception Depth – Not Product Breadth
Market Ownership – Not Market Share
Creativity – Not Duplication
It's YOU – Not The Company

Become Distinct or...Extinct

We are entering a marketing revolution, a revolution that will shift market share, a revolution that will displace the previous success of even some of the most experienced sales professionals, a revolution, that if overlooked, will leave you wondering where to find a new prospect.

Something in the marketplace is changing dramatically. If it takes you much longer to identify the winds of change and to respond accordingly, it will be too late. The damage will be irreversible. The successful sales professional who was the noted *referral getter* of yesterday will eventually not even be able to coerce enough referrals to satisfy the appointments necessary to meet his or her own business and income goals. Success will no longer solely be a factor of getting referrals. Neither will getting adequate appointments for succeeding in your business be solely dependent on being able to make an effective telephone call for an appointment or on blocking out enough time each week to accomplish the goal.

Don Debelak, author of *Marketing Magic*, says, "Every marketer realizes that customers are becoming increasingly difficult to reach." His suggestion, "...you need to figure out a way for your business to gain a sustainable advantage." If you can't capture the prospect's "mindshare" by creating a visible distinction, before the contact is made, your future success will be limited. The sales professionals who want to survive can no longer ignore this market change...NOT THIS TIME!

Ivan R. Misner, Ph.D. and Virginia Devine, authors of *The World's Best Known Marketing Secret,* write, "In today's business environment you need an edge. This means that you need to be very creative in order to be competitive in today's marketplace. Creativity in marketing your business has become a basic tenet for today's successful company or professional practice." Bernd H. Schmitt, the founder and director of Columbia's Marketing Management Executive Program and author of *Experiential Marketing* concurs. He writes, "Today, customers take functional features and benefits, product quality and a positive brand [name] image as a given. What they want is product, communications and marketing campaigns that dazzle their senses, touch their hearts and stimulate their minds. They want all of this to deliver an experience."

Your national home office can't deliver this. You cannot nationally brand an infrequently used intangible service the same way that you can brand a frequently consumed product such as Coca-Cola® and create local customer attraction. Neither can the sales professional achieve the same level of perceived quality guarantee from advertising that a consumable product can attain. The customer knows that quality guarantee has far more to do with the local sales professional and the application of the product or service to their need than it does with the national company name.

What the customer is asking for is *locally driven.* It's all about branding your identity to your local market segment in a visibly unique way. In the near future, those who create a local Identity Brand through consistent familiarization in concert with locally driven, memorable, distinct and unique experiences as compared to the competition will own the prospect. It is not one or the other, but both that will capture the mind of the consumer and provide a competitive edge in selling as well as securing appointments with prospects.

The challenge of your future in the local market place is to become DISTINCT, and not EXTINCT. Chasing the competition with a focus on doing it better or giving better service will be a losing strategy. Marketing can no longer be a fringe consideration for successful sales professionals. Creating a distinct local market identity within your local market segment will become the most major component within your business. It will dictate the extent of your success in the future.

"You're involved in something BIG: the shift to an entirely new economy...a new age...We jeopardize our future if we cling to old assumptions and expectations..." writes Price Pritchett in *New Work Habits For A Radically Changing World.* Marketing in the 21st century will require a strategy transition. Success will require redirecting your primary focus

YOU are a distinct and unique "package of value"...

from getting the prospect to buy to focusing on creating a local prospect perception that YOU are a distinct and unique "package of value," a package of value that is superior to what the local competition, e-commerce or a direct company contact could possibly offer. How well you (not your national company) do in personally creating a superior value perception that creates local customer attraction, *before you have met them,* will determine your future success. Creating a distinct and differentiated local market presence is the only skill that will give you continued and welcomed access to new prospects and provide the continued stream of activity needed to meet your business and financial goals. It is the only appeal that will influence the customer and convince them to allow you to fit into their picture in this "radically changing world...an entirely new economy."

The competitor who is quicker at creating a superior local prospect perception of distinction and differentiation will become your greatest obstacle to surviving tomorrow's complex, competitive marketplace. Having the best product or the highest level of expertise will not be factors in winning over the prospect's mind or in creating a competitive advantage when trying to get in to see the new prospect. The key to your future success will be in attaining continued welcomed access to new prospects within your market who perceive that you are the "mark of excellence – the preferred choice" BEFORE they have ever met you.

Al Ries and Jack Trout write in *Positioning – The Battle For Your Mind,* "Positioning is not what you do to a product. Positioning is what you do to the mind of the prospect." The job will not be to identify groups of potential prospects and figure out ways to convince them to buy your product. The job will be to create a marketing/branding model that attracts the attention of the local prospect and leaves a lasting impression, one of superior value, on their mind. Regis McKenna, author of *Relationship Marketing,* says, "Marketing today is not a function; it is a way of doing business. Marketing is not a new ad campaign or this month's promotion. Marketing has to be all pervasive, part of everyone's job description, from the receptionist to the board of directors."

> *The job will be to create a marketing/branding model that attracts the attention of the local prospect and leaves a lasting impression, one of superior value, on their mind.*

Don't think that adding products or services to your business or practice will help in attracting customers within your market. You may want to diversify your personal investment portfolio but not your business. Diversifying your business in today's market environment should be termed diWORSIFYing. Your market does not view increasing your product breadth as favorable and neither is it seen as smartening up your image nor your local appeal. It is viewed as "dumbing down," not a good strategy for increasing your attractiveness. Logic may be on your side when considering increasing your product offerings. Unfortunately, increased success is not. The greatest successes come to people who focus their energies to narrower markets, provide narrower product offerings and capture a specific market segment. In today's competitive market place, you don't have a product hole to fill; you have a prospect's mind to fill and that is where your primary efforts need to be refocused!

According to Al Ries and Jack Trout in *Positioning - The Battle For Your Mind,* "Today's marketplace is no longer responsive to the strategies that worked in the past. There are just too many products, too many companies, and too much marketing noise." They go on to say, "In the communication jungle out there, the only hope to score big is to be selective, to concentrate on

Marketing is a process, not an event.

narrow targets, to practice segmentation. In a word, positioning." Positioning is no longer secured by developing product or service superiority. It is a psychological sale of perception. Marketing is a process, not an event. Marketing is about developing prospect attraction and relationships, not just orders.

In the future, success will result from becoming effective in creating dialogue, not monologue. Your success begins by building a locally visible, superior value distinction that the consumer sees as your

The more distinctive your identity, the greater your appeal.

Identity Brand, your uniqueness as compared to your competition. Your national corporate home office can't do it for you through national advertising or product development. Customer preference will not be created through new products, product differentiation, 800 numbers, Web sites or annual customer survey forms. You will secure your success by

Identity Branding YOU. And the more distinctive your identity, the greater your appeal to your market segments.

Regis McKenna, author of *Relationship Marketing,* says that unlike the revolutionary products developed in the 1950s and 1960s such as the Weber Charcoal Grill and the color TV, products no longer

market positioning is created in the mind

"suddenly appear in our midst and overwhelm us." Product is no longer the driving element for dominating a market segment. Local market creativity is. Why? Because products don't create market positioning when the consumer views them as essentially all equal. McKenna says, "To succeed in the future, marketers will have to learn new and better ways of bringing value to the customer." Today, market positioning is created in the mind of the consumer, not in the product development room. What actually gets driven into the mind today is not the product. It is YOU.

Positioning is no longer the result of selling superior products or offering better service. Positioning starts with an experience. For the prospect, that experience is the beginning of a perception. The experience is not initiated in an opening interview; it is initiated before the prospect ever meets you. Perception is the basis for building a competitive advantage, an Identity Brand. Its foundation is not created out of logic, common sense or working harder. It's built out of creativity. The following chapters will provide a guide for your future success, a guide to lead you through this next marketing revolution, a guide to help you build an Identity Brand, YOU, that eventually becomes the mark of excellence within your market segment.

McGraw-Hill had an advertisement in the past that read:

I don't know who you are.
I don't know your company.
I don't know your company's product.
I don't know your company's customers.
I don't know your company's record.
I don't know your company's reputation.
Now—what was it you wanted to sell me?

MORAL: *Sales start before your salesman calls.*

IDENTITY BRANDING

IDENTITY BRANDING

How Did We Get Here?

IDENTITY BRANDING

Marketing Is Misunderstood

Until the 1970's, America was a country that had never felt the effects of inflation. Wages hadn't changed much for over twenty years. People lived in neighborhoods where they not only knew each other but they socialized together. Their children started walking to school together in kindergarten and graduated from high school with those same friends. The new kid in school was a novelty. Very rarely did anyone move. Business was transacted on a handshake. New products took a long time to produce. Infomercials did not exist, most people were buying their first color TV and, prior to 1973, NO ONE had ever received a telemarketing call.

Junk-mail didn't exist; neither did credit cards. Credit was still a novelty, which, if available, was set up with your local men's or women's clothing store that billed you at the end of the month, when, on the rare occasion, you used it. Carhops delivering hamburgers far outnumbered the few McDonald's restaurants that had been constructed. Television had only three channels. There were no remote controls and the TV repairman still came to your home. Divorce was scandalous and rare. Being cheated in a business deal was almost unheard of. The "Ozzie and Harriet" life style was, to a large extent, REAL! But not anymore. You are about to witness the most profound marketing change that has ever affected America. Some will survive. Many will not. Your survival will depend on how well informed you are and the actions that you choose to take. Choose them wisely!

You are about to witness the most profound marketing change that has ever affected America.

The Consumer Wants to Know "Why You?"

Michael Boylan, author of *The Power to Get In,* says, "The rules of the game of getting in have changed drastically. In order to get in the door today, you've got to trash your old strategies, tactics and methods and learn to do things differently." Success is no longer a selling game. It is not even a prospecting game. It is a marketing game. Marketing is not about strong-arming your way into the prospect's door. It is not even about identifying multiple prospects that need and can afford your offering and then making an effective approach for an initial appointment. It is not about becoming resilient to the first "no," learning the newest answers to objections and then pushing a little harder for a "yes." Marketing is not selling. Marketing is not prospecting. Marketing is about getting the prospect attracted to you before the first contact is initiated. It is about getting prospects to knowingly want you to contact them.

Success is no longer a selling game.

Marketing is not selling. Marketing is not prospecting. Marketing is about getting the prospect attracted to you before the first contact is initiated.

In the professional service industries, the marketing challenge won't be met through your company's national advertising and promotion campaign. It is a local challenge whose orchestration belongs to you. It is all about how to create a personal local market presence that attracts the prospect and answers their question, "Why you?"

The Prospect Has Changed and Why YOU Will Have to Respond

Marketing is, perhaps, the most misunderstood element in corporate America today. It is especially misunderstood in the service industries that sell intangible products or services that are purchased but are then infrequently used or revisited such as insurance, mutual funds, stocks and legal services. Many corporate executives argue that their company is different. Their clients receive quarterly corporate communications and frequently see the company's name in its newest TV ad, sponsored national sporting event and in print publications. Why is it that such companies have paid large sums of money to their advertising firms and can produce proof that their name has higher public recognition than last year, yet their distribution professionals are fighting harder to just "get-in?"

professionals are fighting harder to just "get-in"

The sales professionals know that something has changed. They know that they are working harder. They know that the prospect is more resistant than ever before to the initial request for an interview. They find themselves now, no different than the average consumer, hanging up on telemarketers and being angered by the continued onslaught of junk-mail and solicitations. The consumer is angry and discouraged, and so is the salesperson who has mistakenly built their career on the wrong business model. This critical mistake shows in the ranks of many of the older veterans. Once enthusiastic, energetic and highly successful sales professionals who used to extend a hearty welcome to new associates, now watch almost silently as the new rookie enters their profession with the knowledge that fewer "make it" today than in the past. They still wish them the best, though more quietly now, knowing all too well the narrowing odds against success and the discouragement that these new associates may face. They wish, for their own benefit as well as for the new associate, that the old days would return, when they were more motivated and prospects were easier to access.

Many of the veterans are discouraged and worn out. Building their business foundation on a selling model instead of a marketing model has taken its toll. Even those who have been successful in their careers by placing their emphasis on selling, being a great closer or knowing how to compel people to make a buying decision know that something is missing. Maybe it's a lack of personal fulfillment with their careers. Whatever you believe it to be, that lack of something has caused enthusiasm to wane, motivation to be lost and burnout to cause many to seek new careers.

Today, for people to feel fulfilled and satisfied not only in their personal lives but also equally in their business lives calls for meaning, community and authentication. They want to feel assured that what they do is important, to feel that they belong and to physically hear, not just from their manager but more importantly from their prospect community, continued affirmations of appreciation for what they give and who they are. When those three elements, meaning, community and continual authentication, aren't present in sufficient quantity, people leave relationships as well as successful careers either physically or mentally.

Building a new business model for the future, based on marketing and not selling, will not only be necessary for successfully reaching the customer in the near future, but it will be necessary to sustain the success and the retention of the professional salesperson. By delivering the three elements of meaning, community and authentication back into the sales profession, you will see careers renewed, retention ratios of both new and experienced sales professionals increase and attraction increase, not only for the consumer but also for candidates considering a career in professional sales.

We Were a Product Driven Industry

Until the early 1970s, the insurance industry was a product driven industry. In 1970, the average consumer had less than $14,000 of life insurance coverage. The only distinction between policy types was that insurance companies structured as mutual companies issued participating policies (called par policies) and insurance companies structured as stock companies issued nonparticipating (called nonpar policies). Participating policies paid dividends. Nonparticipating policies did not pay dividends, but they were usually twenty-five percent less expensive. As an agent, one was taught, when in competition, how to destroy the competing type of contract. Mutual companies trained their agents that stock companies paid all of their profits to their stockholders and therefore the policyholder would eventually get left out, a serious disadvantage. Stock companies trained their agents to emphasize that the IRS called dividends from mutual life insurance policies a return of premium and that was why they were tax-free. Agents were told to emphasize to the prospect, "Why would you want to pay an overcharge to your insurance company in order to get your own money back at a later date?"

Though the agents from these two different type companies were archrivals, almost everyone considered policy replacement to be unethical. Many agents prided themselves upon having been in the business for years without ever replacing a policy. They all supported their life underwriters associations and shared sales ideas willingly. Why? Because no one was doing anything different, plus "proselytizing" (stealing agents from another company) was regarded as unethical as policy replacement. Either act would incur an invitation to appear before an ethics board where one would be reprimanded and warned that another occurrence could result in expulsion from the organization.

People Were Easy to Access

There were plenty of prospects in the 1960s and '70s. Recruiting new agents was not difficult and, comparatively speaking, neither was getting an appointment with a prospect. People were gracious. If someone hung up on you, you were taught to call them back and apologize that somehow you must have been cut off by the telephone company. Believe it or not, you could usually continue the conversation with no one admitting any differently. A certain respect and etiquette between people was still alive and well within our society. Once you got in to see the prospect, everyone used the same sales talk, "You'll Earn a Fortune," and it produced results.

Agents were taught to sell on a one-interview approach. There were no ledger illustrations. There were only pocket rate books that contained the numbers necessary for calculating premiums, the guaranteed cash values and dividend values for providing a quote. Rate books could easily last two or three years before updating was necessary. In the early 1970s, some agents would eventually order sample ledgers, which would take five to ten days to receive from the home office. Because of the time element, multiple illustrations for prospects with ages at five-year increments, such as ages twenty-five through age fifty-five, were often ordered for creating a sales illustration book. The illustrations were ordered for $25,000, $50,000 and $100,000 insurance face-amounts and would be used in selling interviews. There was no need for any other amounts. This was a product sale and the average client was sold a $25,000 whole-life policy with guaranteed purchase options for future increases. Term insurance was expensive, really expensive after the third year, and seldom posed a problem in competition. Flexible premium contracts such as universal life had not been invented and terms such as unit cost and return on equity (ROE) were unheard of. Even Ward Cleaver ("Leave It to Beaver's" dad) was proudly portrayed as an insurance agent whom you never saw working past six p.m. and must have lived off of his renewals (that is my guess). Life was pretty good but "change" was starting to stir things up. Some agents would adjust, others would lament the good old days and fade away.

Needs-Analysis Replaces the Product Sale

Sometime around the early 1970s, a need analysis sales approach, called *Capital Needs Analysis,* which is attributable to Tom Wolfe, was catching on in the insurance industry. The buying public was changing. Consumers were developing an increased desire to know more before purchasing anything. This generation, the boomers, was better educated than any previous generation. They were watching more TV and advertisements were filling the channels. All of this contributed to a major selling change.

> *The buying public was changing. Consumers were developing an increased desire to know more.*

The 1950s ushered in the birth of modern America with its continued appetite for space exploration (NASA). The technological marvels that took us to the moon were now making an impact on American consumers with companies responding with new products and divisions established for research and development. Landing on the moon was the catalyst for a new emphasis on learning and education. People were told that they were in charge of their own destinies. The large manufacturing companies that had dominated employment in America were starting to change. They were confronting more competition and needed to respond by becoming more competitive. Ending their defined-benefit pension plans, that so many employees had considered as almost a God-given right and depended on for their retirement security, was an expense that many companies determined they could no longer continue. Inflation and then stagflation (high inflation and low unemployment) were ravaging fixed incomes and corporate profits. Housing prices were soaring, as was the cost of everything else. Mutual funds were just being created and a recession would soon create shock waves that would see stockbrokers jumping out of windows and the adult population grasping for answers. To add to the frustration level of

19

many families to whom change had been so rare, the baby boomers were, on almost any subject, no longer willing to accept with blind faith many of the traditional beliefs that their parents had always held about life in general.

This new generation was starting to complete college in numbers never before seen and the beginning of the computer age had emerged. The medical courses in college were no longer the only major that had 24-hour open labs; the students in the Fortran computer classes now joined them. The adults were fully aware that these graduating kids had more education than they did.

They were willing to listen...to the college graduate ...and extend to them an elevated trust that will forever remain unique to this time in history.

Computers had ushered in a new knowledge level with a new language that few understood, yet almost all respected. Middle age and older adults were more than willing to listen, with admiration, to the college graduate who was twenty-five to forty years younger than they and to extend to them an elevated trust that will forever remain unique to this time in history.

The insurance product sale of yesterday, usually sold as a packaged amount, was being replaced with an individual calculation of death and retirement needs. Hand-held calculators by Texas Instruments were selling in 1974 for $119, which to everyone's amazement dropped almost immediately in price to $49.95 and then to $19.95 over the next year. Computers, albeit with limited functionality, would appear on the scene by the mid-to-late 1970s. Prospects and clients would see the numbers scroll off of the computer screen. They would actually stand up and look behind the computer as if the numbers were on a scrolling roll of paper. Salespersons would learn to answer their questions of "Where do the numbers go?" without making them feel foolish.

No one had ever mailed in a request for a social security audit of his or her benefits much less had a calculation performed to integrate these benefits

> *the public was tired of being sold product...*

within a needs-analysis plan. This was "high-level" planning and consumers were fascinated, interested and receptive. It is no wonder that so many young persons entered the insurance industry straight out of college and succeeded. The 1970s saw a technology/education gap emerge between the generations that created a preference for youth, instead of experience, that has never been replicated. The new college graduate was seen as intelligent and capable of providing information that was out of reach for the older generation. The older generation welcomed them in advisory capacities in spite of their youth. In addition, the public was tired of being sold product with no explanation. They wanted to know "WHY" and a more sophisticated

> *The agent who resisted this change was soon left behind, a fact worth remembering.*

needs-analysis approach was the new door opener. The agent who resisted this change was soon left behind, a fact worth remembering.

The Consultative Approach Enters the Scene

The focus on needs-analysis remained strong but made a subtle yet substantial change in the late 1970s and early 1980s. The Xerox Selling Skills course had revolutionized the selling industry. It was used in the insurance industry, as was the Wilson Learning Skills program, to teach agents how to conduct a consultative approach in dealing with the "new" consumer.

> *the consumer...wanted less judgment extended and more listening.*

Consumers had changed again. They no longer wanted someone to just gather objective information and return with a needs-analysis. They wanted a sense of dealing with a consultant. They wanted to know that their opinions counted. More than objective facts mattered. Subjective feelings mattered as well, maybe even more. The philosophy expressed in the book, *"I'm OK, You're OK"* was reflective of the rise of the consumer who wanted less judgment extended and more listening. They wanted their feelings to be taken into consideration. Risk tolerance questionnaires began to enter the sales process; this new consultative approach required a minimum of two interviews with the prospect before being able to make a product recommendation. The one interview sales approach was quickly fading from the scene.

The financial planning era, along with "financial advisors" (a new identifying name), dawned in the mid-1980s. It would develop quickly with financial advisors promoting tax shelters for reducing the taxes for their clientele. The tax brackets were at the highest level the country had ever seen. These were the same ninety percent tax brackets that provided a political platform for Ronald Reagan to run for President of the United States. However, the tax shelters would eventually threaten the credibility of the whole industry as the IRS would challenge, disallow the tax deduction and charge penalties of up to fifty percent plus interest on the original deduction. In addition, most of the investments never returned even the principal investment to the investor, much less any profit. They lost it all!

The age of skepticism was beginning to have an impact...

Universal life was being promoted with interest rates of up to sixteen to eighteen percent with cash values projected out for thirty years, forty years and sometimes more. Policy replacement of old contracts was rampant. Some companies even replaced their own client contracts to try to prevent the competition from getting to them first. Enough was enough. The industry started making attempts to regulate their own member companies but not in time to keep a major weekly national magazine from putting its well-remembered commentary on the front cover. A chimpanzee dressed like a professor, sitting on a stool, holding a piece of chalk towards a blackboard filled with numbers had a caption that read (something like), "Seems like anyone can call themselves a Financial Planner." The age of skepticism was beginning to have an impact on the financial service's industry.

The New Client Expects a Partnership Approach

By the 1990s, the new client wanted more than just a consultant who listened during an initial approach interview and then returned with an analysis and recommendation. They wanted to be included in the decision-making process for determining solutions. They knew that there were multiple ways to approach a financial plan. The recommendation process was no longer sacred. It would become participatory. This was the advent of giving multiple-choice recommendations or partnering on the computer and allowing the prospect to feel like they were involved.

The proliferation of industry products had created parity in the eyes of the consumer. The industry had matured. The consumer believed that all companies had all products. If anyone had a competitive advantage, it would not last for long. The consumer no longer believed "Best." Best was a relative term. Product was no longer the driving force in the consumer's decision to make a purchase. The driving force was what the consumer viewed as the "package of value," which was much more than product and price.

Consumer Commonality Becomes a Core Value

In the early 1990s this era of partnership was quickly enhanced with a focus on "value commonality." The market place had once again changed and the new theory was that people would prefer to do business with those with whom they shared common values. This theory was the catalyst for encouraging sales people to target their selling activity to specific affinity groups to which they were legitimately attracted. The belief was that people who shared a common cause or who shared a common core value were more apt to grant an appointment and transact business. Salespeople were told to find their market niche, focus and work their sales plan, but something was missing.

> *...original marketing programs were little more than group identification programs.*

Some organizations hired consultants to help their sales professionals learn how to market. In hindsight, most of these original marketing programs were little more than group identification programs. They lacked substance when it came to advising what to do once the financial advisor "arrived." The so-called marketing plans these consultants did promote were still based on a selling model, not a marketing model. They promoted ideas such as getting the names of the group members and sending wave mailings (a staggered mailing of three letters over three weeks) with a follow-up phone call requesting an interview. By now, if one didn't look like an outsider to the group, this proved it!

The focus was still on what the sales professional could "get," a sale, versus what he could "give." The results did not deliver what was expected. Some sales professionals were all but run out of groups. They knew that they had tarnished their reputations within this group, no matter how sincerely their efforts had begun. Some sales professionals made limited sales, but this was not marketing.

Companies and their sales people had great expectations for the success of these original marketing plans. They knew that the traditional methods weren't working. Retention had fallen to an all-time industry low. Sales per distribution unit were down and continued to decrease. "Getting in" was harder and every sale professional knew it. They were led to believe that marketing was the solution. The theory was right. The methods were wrong.

Marketing, or better yet, Identity Branding, is about creating the future. Its purpose is to create favorable prospect attraction before the prospect has met you and well in advance of your first approach asking for an appointment. It is about building a prospect highway to a sizable prospect community that embraces you, one that can be traveled indefinitely. It is about producing a higher sense of fulfillment for the sales professional, a more assured way to build on his success. It is about creating a prospect preference, one that welcomes you to make the initial interview request. The goal in Identity Branding is to build a relationship whose foundation is created before your first encounter, which creates a win-win situation for everyone.

Many companies, agencies and sales associates are still trying to make a marketing plan based on a selling model work. The result will be a continued disappointment until this basic mistake is corrected. Someone once said that if you are headed in the wrong direction, the last

Marketing, or better yet, Identity Branding, is about... building a prospect highway to a sizable prospect community that embraces you, one that can be traveled indefinitely.

thing you want to do is to arrive there quicker. The directions and foundations of most of these plans are simply wrong.

The market place has changed. Marketing is not group identification and success is no longer a selling game. Marketing is about "getting the consumer to notice you FIRST." It is about getting the prospect

Marketing is about "getting the consumer to notice you FIRST."

attracted to you before the contact is initiated. It is about getting them to want you to contact them. The wants and needs of the consumer today may be similar to what they were ten years

IDENTITY BRANDING

ago, but their ways of wanting to be approached and handled are dramatically different. If you don't know the new rules, your efforts will fail. Though your plans may be called "marketing," if their foundation is flawed you will meet with discouragement. There is a better way.

26

IDENTITY BRANDING

Networking, Finding Prospects and Capturing "Mindshare"

IDENTITY BRANDING

This Market Change Must Not Be Ignored

Something in the marketplace is changing dramatically. If it takes you much longer to identify the winds of change and to respond accordingly, it will be too late. The damage will be irreversible. The successful *referral getter* of yesterday will eventually be unable to even coerce enough referrals to satisfy the appointments necessary to meet his own income needs. Success will no longer solely be a factor of getting referrals. Neither will getting adequate numbers of appointments for succeeding in our business be solely dependent on being able to make an effective telephone call for an appointment or on blocking out enough time each week to accomplish the goal. If you can't capture the prospect's "mindshare" before the contact is made, your future success will be limited. Those who want to survive can no longer ignore market change.

Accessibility to Prospects Has Decreased

A consumer marketing revolution, already underway, will continue to decrease your accessibility to prospects. Even the faces of yesterday's highly successful sales professionals may eventually fade away. To prevent this from happening to you, marketing must not become just another item added to your business plan. It must become your business plan. A marketing model, not a selling model, must become the driving force of your business if you are to confront this new marketing revolution successfully.

Success is no longer a game of courage contingent upon whether you can make a successful cold call. It is a marketing game. Marketing is not about strong-arming your way into the prospect's door or building up a "thick skin" to withstand rejection and continuing to persevere. You must learn to navigate among an entirely new world of prospects or the shifting currents will eventually crush your ship. A change to the marketplace has arrived. No matter how successful you have been in the past, if you don't adjust to this change, you will suffer the unpleasant consequences that lie in wait.

The New Rules For "Getting In"

Harry Hoopis, leading general agent with Northwestern Mutual in Chicago says, "The phone has reached the level of diminishing returns. The more you use it, the less time you have to sell. It takes sixty dials per day to do what we use to do with ten dials per day. There aren't enough hours in the day to continue this trend." Michael Boylan says, in *The Power to Get In,* "The rules of the game of getting in have changed drastically. In order to get in the door today, you've got to trash your old strategies, tactics and methods and learn to do things differently." Boylan continues, "...many of your desired prospects don't want to see or talk with you. If they did, you could pick up the phone and schedule all the appointments you wanted." The bottom line is that you can ignore the signs and do nothing while your market access problem worsens, and it will, or you can take a different approach and watch the market access door open wider to you while it closes further to the competition that remains unenlightened.

To win in this new environment, you will need to successfully accomplish two things. First, you must find a specific market(s) segment focus that possesses two criteria. It

> *...you will need to successfully accomplish two things...find a specific market(s) segment focus...and construct an arrival action plan*

must be suitable and it must emotionally pull your interest. Secondly you must construct an arrival action plan so that when you get market active you can become identified by the prospect as distinctively different from the competition.

What Market Will You Target?

The first element that must be addressed is what market you will target. Dr. Thomas Stanley, in his book *Networking With The Affluent,* says, "Too few sales professionals target effectively." Most sales professionals and companies think they are targeting because they can give a generic targeting description, such as small business owners, for their focus. That description is simply too general! If the truth were known, most sales professionals are still contacting any referral they are given (especially by their largest clients) as long as they feel they can get a

> *Most sales professionals and companies think they are targeting because they can give a generic targeting description, such as small business owners, for their focus. That description is simply too general!*

"respectable size check," which they proudly acknowledge as larger than that of most of their less experienced peers. This is hardly the idea of marketing. Their efforts are more similar to a continual hunting expedition. Their resilience may be commendable, but this type of focus eventually wears out even the most committed.

Identifying an affinity group, such as homebuilders or occupational therapists, that you may want to target is important, but simply identifying a group is not marketing. It is only the initial step in positioning. It is comparable to a lumberjack standing at night between the city lights and the forest in an initial attempt to decide which direction to head in the morning. His initial conclusion should give him a good sense of direction as to which way he should go in the morning to get to his *group of trees,* but nothing more.

What Is an Effective Market Segment?

Professional salespersons do not survive when they continue to view the entire world as their market. However, unless their product line is user specific to a very narrow group of consumers, neither do they normally focus entirely on only one segment of individuals. Most sales professionals will have one to three, three usually being the maximum, well-defined and identifiable groups that they consider their primary market and to which they focus their attention. After you have thought through who in your personal sphere (i.e., friends, acquaintances, fellow church members, civic club associates) should be included in your market and your efforts to Identity Brand your reputation, you will need to determine where your prospect highway to a larger prospect community needs to be constructed. This will vary from one individual to another and from one geographical area to another. You may find welcomed access in one city and resistance in another. Once you have decided on the market segment(s) that you want to concentrate on, your efforts should now be focused on individualizing your market by identifying names for inclusion into your *Prospect Fishbowl*™.

There should be two primary components present in selecting a market segment before putting a great effort into individualizing your market by attaining specific prospect names and then beginning the process to Identity Brand your reputation. The first component should be consideration of size. Considering that it will take a dedication of effort to become distinctly positioned as the brand of choice, you will want to be assured that your efforts are impacting an adequate number of prospects necessary to meet your goals. It will take as much effort to influence a group of fifty people as it would a group of five hundred. Considering that you are limited by the number of hours for this task, if you know that you will need to influence a thousand prospects over the next few years, don't get involved with a group of fewer than two hundred people.

The number two component for finding an appropriate market segment is that the sales professional must have an affinity for or share a commonality to it. If you don't like the people or the cause, don't attempt to build a prospect highway to the group. You will never be able to identify or communicate well to it. Don't get attracted solely by prestige or net worth. Yes, they need to be able to afford whatever you are offering; however, you must find a group that you share a commonality with and one that you genuinely like. Simply stated, find a kindred spirit.

Here is a market segment definition for consideration in focusing your thoughts:

A market should be an identifiable segment of people who knowingly share a significant commonality, which may be based on:

- *Occupation*

- *A deep dedication to a special interest (usually hobbies, recreation or clubs)*

- *A significant involvement with a community or a civic organization*

- *An organized, deeply shared social cause*

- *A life-defining religious following*

- *A cohesive ethnic group*

who regularly network and communicate with each other.

When I find a professional salesperson who is attempting to market to a defined market segment, who has a well thought through marketing plan but is struggling with attaining results, I normally find that the market definition has been compromised or their personal commonality to the segment is weak, possibly nonexistent. We will discuss that further in the next few pages.

Individualize Your Market

Choosing an appropriate market segment is the beginning step in deciding toward whom to direct your efforts. However, as Lynn Upshaw says, in *Building Brand Identity,* "Smart brand marketers rethink who their targets are by acknowledging that they are not targets at all, but individual human beings." He believes that you must "individualize" the future customer [prospect] not as a group but as a person. You must know by name those whom you want to influence, those from whom you want to capture "mindshare" over the next months and years. Then you must increase their familiarization with you.

> *...you must "individualize" the future customer [prospect] not as a group but as a person.*

Ford Harding, in his book *Creating Rainmakers,* defines rainmakers as those professionals who have an uncanny ability to create leads and sales results that are far superior to the other professionals in their firms. As individuals, the main element of their success is expressed as, "The rainmakers never lost track of a client or prospective client or other important contact. Once they develop a relationship with someone, they never let go." He further states, "...rainmakers build big networks...and...strive to stay in front of their network members' minds." Because of this constant one-to-one familiarization, these people eventually become clients; the sales professional knows exactly whom to cultivate, whom to direct their *Identity Branding* efforts to, whom to send newsletters to, whom to consistently invite to events. These super achievers built a foundational *Prospect Fishbowl* of at least 1,000 prospects and then focused their attention to adding, nurturing, and learning to migrate (versus prospect) among the individuals in a way that the individuals appreciated. Their primary focus changes from prospecting to maintaining continual familiarization (migrating within their *Prospect Fishbowl*) by providing value in order to capture "mindshare," which in turn creates prospect attraction.

> *These super achievers built a foundational Prospect Fishbowl of at least 1,000 prospects...*

A thought-provoking commentary on rainmakers was written in the January 10, 2000 edition of *Forbes* magazine. The article, authored by Robert Lenzner and Ashlea Ebeling, was titled *"A Wealth of Names-David Rockefeller Sr. is the ultimate rainmaker."* The article begins, "You can measure David Rockefeller Sr.'s wealth and power by taking a look at his stock portfolio, his real estate holdings or his art collection. Or you can take an elevator to the 56th floor of Rockefeller Center in New York and look for an alcove that encloses a massive Ferris wheel of a Rolodex. This 4-foot-by-5-foot contraption is the fulcrum of Rockefeller's globe-trotting life at the age of 84." The Rolodex contains 150,000 names. Is it any wonder why David Rockefeller Sr. is perhaps the number-one money raiser for philanthropic causes in the world today, much less why he was and still is a world tycoon of a businessperson? The article calls his Rolodex, "a working man's toolbox" and finishes with "That Rolodex is worth a fortune...but you can't put a value on it."

> *The Rolodex contains 150,000 names.*
>
> *"That Rolodex is worth a fortune...but you can't put a value on it."*

As you consider your efforts in individualizing your prospect market, remember the lesson from David Rockefeller Sr. He never could have attained the success in his endeavors without knowing his prospects by name. A general description of a market segment would never have supported Rockefeller's accomplishments, and neither will it for you. You probably don't need 150,000 names to meet your goals, but you will need more than your closest one hundred friends, your list of two hundred clients or the remaining thirty-five referrals that you have stacked on your desk to call on.

What to Do Once You Get Market Active

Once you identify the market segment(s) that you believe you want to focus your efforts towards, you would be ill-advised to start your marketing by sending multiple sales solicitation letters (often called wave-mails) to the members and then calling for an appointment. You would have more failure than success. Why? Because this technique will verify to the membership that you are an *"outsider."* Why would you need to send a solicitation letter to a colleague if you were an *"insider"* who had the group's respect? You have ruined the perception that you have the group's deep concerns as part of your interest. Their perception will be that your interest in regard to their cause is not genuine, has no real emotional connection and neither is it a life-long commitment. The perception is that you are here *"to get"* and not *"to give."* Your multiple letter-mailing programs within a cohesive market segment will either fail miserably or after it has resulted in some minor successes, you will be well aware that you have worn out your welcome and your future success in this group will be limited. You will now need to find a new group and start the process all over again. So much for solicitation letters being the solution to solving your life-long prospecting and market access problems. This is an unfortunate story that has been repeated far too many times within our industry.

The sales professional who joins a group and after numerous years has developed a limited number of clients within the group also has a brand personality problem. Most likely, they still feel awkward, almost embarrassed, to request an interview with another group member in hopes of beginning a business relationship. Just ask a sales professional. In an environment where they can safely talk, they will verify this. The issue is not whether they are missing opportunities in front of their noses; the issue is why has it been so difficult to transition prospects into clients. They know that they have developed no prospect business preference although they may have been involved with this group for years. They have never had an adequate marketing plan that was structured to direct their "what to do" efforts once they arrived. They are like the lumberjack who knew the general direction to travel to get to the forest but didn't know what to do once he arrived.

We have a marketing problem and an arrival problem within this industry. In a mature industry built on a selling model and not a marketing model, once the consumers believed that they were generally well acquainted with the product, what else could you expect to develop but a market access problem? The novelty of the product or service would no longer suffice for getting in the door.

We have a marketing problem and an arrival problem within this industry.

The financial industry, as a whole, has placed more emphasis on getting new associates off to a fast start (selling) than on creating a foundational market. The frustration and challenge this has created are comparable to asking the sales associate to "change a tire on a moving car." The task is almost impossible, but even if successfully completed the first few times, you can only imagine the

The...challenge...(is) comparable to asking the sales associate to "change a tire on a moving car."

frustration created. Most people eventually give up, especially as the car travels so much faster today than yesterday.

The psychological elements necessary for an individual to sustain motivation are based on behavior requested and the consequences incurred. If positive consequences are not incurred in adequate numbers as to the behavior being requested, the individual will eventually curtail the activity, if not stop entirely. When the only positive consequence of a fast-start selling endeavor is an immediate "sale," you will more than likely have inadequate successes to sustain most people's motivation. On the other hand, if the fast-start behavior were redefined to accumulating names and building impressions to a defined prospect community, numerous activities on a daily basis could be defined as success and motivation would be sustained until the market were receptive to the professional's contact. Until the industry starts emphasizing building a substantial individualized prospect foundation, before focusing their emphasis on getting the sales associate off to a fast (selling) start, we will continue to see eroding retention and senior agents who after ten, fifteen, or twenty years, still don't understand marketing.

It is no wonder that insurance agents and financial advisors are leaving their parent companies and agencies to become affiliated with banks or even competing organizations that have a perceived "higher profile." The perception is that these organizations have a greater client "mind-share" and that it is easier to get in front of the prospect. The manager's response has been, "But you're losing ownership of your block of business! Look at all you are giving up." The agents' and financial advisors' response, though normally not verbalized, has been, "No...You don't understand. Look at all I am gaining." It is not the competition that is affecting you. The marketing revolution is affecting you! If you don't address the marketing issue, your problems will get worse.

If you don't address the marketing issue, your problems will get worse.

Call Reluctance Can Increase

If the sale professionals involved in specific market segments were successful in Identity Branding themselves as the "mark of excellence" within their field, I believe that call reluctance would eventually be replaced with call enthusiasm. They would eventually sense that they own the market because of the value they have given. However, until that happens, they will be reluctant to initiate a selling contact while not really knowing how the group perceives them, as an *insider* or an *outsider*. To compound the problem, after a while they will have established friends within the group. If they don't know how their contact for business will be received, they won't initiate a call. It is much harder on the sales professional to be turned down by a friend than it is by a stranger. Although they may not have achieved business "mindshare," they have made friends. Their friendship, with the development of no market preference, no "mindshare," will emotionally stop their well-planned intentions to call on these people whom they originally targeted.

If networking provides so much, why is it that networking is such an anomaly to so many sales professionals and managers? It is one of the most critical items for effective marketing and it is critical to the success of most sales professionals. However, it is seldom done. My conclusion is that networking is one of the most misunderstood items within all selling professions. Not only is it done poorly, the purpose is usually improperly defined. Those two elements alone render it practically impossible to attain great results. So let's start by defining the purpose of networking and then defining how to do it.

The Purpose of Networking

Initially, networking's purpose is to meet significant groups of potential prospects with the intention of being able to *"give,"* not *"get."*

In today's age of consumer skepticism, if your intention is to meet people so that you can "get" instead of "give," your success will be limited. People prefer to buy from people whom they perceive as

if your intention is to... "get" instead of "give," your success will be limited.

popular, someone with a distinct reputation. You cannot become popular by meeting someone and then immediately telling them about yourself while attempting to get what you want instead of providing what they want. Effective networking begins by asking about them. If done properly, networking can become your number-one way to accumulate prospect names for your *Prospect Fishbowl*, persons you will then want to influence and cultivate with value information delivered uniquely over time. Eventually, networking's primary purpose will change from building an abundance of qualified prospect names to deepening the "mindshare" of the identified prospects. However, you will always be on the alert to find new prospects to replace your less desirable ones as your *Prospect Fishbowl* evolves through your success and your increasing skill level.

Research among the leading sales professionals indicates that your *Prospect Fishbowl* should have a minimum of 1,000 names (2,000 is better!). The nationally known financial service company, Edward Jones Investments, best illustrates the results that this can incur. Edward Jones Investments has one of the highest retention ratios for sales professionals in the industry, over eighty-five percent for first-year sales associates and over seventy percent for fifth-year sales associates. Compare that to an industry retention ratio of between eleven to fifteen percent! It is reported that their average income for fifth-year sales professionals exceeds $150,000. Because they expect an associate to build an inventory of approximately 1,500 prospects and to have personally met all of them within their first three to six months, is it any wonder why their retention and success ratios are so high?

The Edward Jones new representative's main focus for four months is to meet twenty-five prospects per day, Monday through Saturday, with an objective to initiate a relationship rather than an immediate sale. That initial meeting provides the representative with the prospect's permission to begin the process of familiarization through future educational mailings and invitations to investment events. Representatives build an initial prospect foundation to which they can focus their efforts to consistently familiarize themselves to individuals, not just to a generic target market. These initial daily contacts result in providing frequent positive feedback, which creates emotional building blocks that sustains the representative's motivation and confidence.

Success is not defined by, nor dependent on making a sale. The representative's motivation is sustained from the daily positive prospect contacts and from knowing that their present efforts are cultivating the fields of their future success. The Edward Jones Company helps lay solid marketing foundations for their sales associates and they don't veer from their structure. If you want to do it another way, find another firm. It won't be Edward Jones.

The Edward Jones Investment Company, along with Wal-Mart and Southwest Airlines, is currently a curriculum case study in the Harvard School of Business because of their high level of success with their customers and their sales organization. One Harvard professor is said to frequently comment that the Edward Jones Company appears to have been designed by the customer. I am sure that the Edward Jones Company focus, on providing consistent value information to identified individual prospects, makes the prospects and clients feel that these Edward Jones representatives are focused on *giving* first and *getting* second, the basis for a business that attracts customers.

To be a successful networker your actions must convey that your networking activities are about the prospect and not for telling about yourself. Marketing and networking require consistency, no different

> *Marketing is...about providing value, eventually capturing "mindshare"*

than achieving a health-fitness goal. It takes patience and perseverance. Most agents give up on marketing efforts way too prematurely, and with the companies emphasis on fast sales results, it's almost impossible to refocus them back on marketing and on developing a prospect foundation before a career crisis sets in. Getting a sale is certainly part of what a selling profession is all about, but it is initially the wrong focus for the agents first few months and the low industry retention ratio proves it. Marketing is not about meeting people to see what you can get from them within the shortest possible time frame. It is about providing value, eventually capturing "mindshare" and creating consumer preference, which then provides market access to people wanting to see you.

How to Begin Networking

So, how do you get started? If I were an experienced sale professional, I would start with identifying my most successful clients, whom I would clone numerous times, if I could. If I were a new associate, I would start by identifying friends and acquaintances whom I would like to have as clients and if I could replicate them a hundred times over, I would. I would identify three of my best, make an appointment, tell them how highly I think of them and explain my purpose. I would tell them that I am specializing my "practice" by narrowing my market focus to three affinity groups within which I want to concentrate the majority of my work. I would explain that I was hoping they might assist me in accomplishing that goal. Ask them what occupational associations they belong to and start there. It is fine if you need to use a questionnaire of sorts (refer to available resources in the back of the book), but make sure that they realize that you are asking questions to determine what you can give and not what you can get.

Be practical. If you don't want to work with schoolteachers, don't initiate a marketing conversation with one. Start with individuals whom you believe represent an industry that has both sufficient quantity and financial promise. Don't get discouraged if, as you get more information, you find that your group has limited potential. Choosing a market segment to target is not an exact science; rather, it is much more like selling. Sometimes you will be fooled. Parker Palmer, author of *Let Your Life Speak,* says that in life as in any experiment, "negative results are at least as important as successes." Don't let a false start discourage you. You will learn a lot even from a failure should you experience one. Just expect that one out of three times your initiative to get involved with a market segment group will be wrong, so find another group and try again. Trust that your perseverance will be rewarded.

Some groups you may want to consider as potential market segments are homebuilders, general contractors, home remodelers, building material supply associations, HVAC contractors, plumbers, electricians, pest control associations, automobile dealer associations, printers, human resource associations, snack food vendors, forest farmers, lumber companies, dairy farmers, poultry farmers and suppliers, restaurant associations and restaurant suppliers, furniture manufacturers, textile manufacturers, United Arts Council, The National Association of Christians and Jews, and even coaches of local youth soccer, baseball and basketball teams. The list can go on forever! For your local associations, look in the *Associations Yellow Book* or the *Gale Encyclopedia of Associations* at your local library. It will list them all and will also provide a lot of information to help you evaluate your initial choices.

Write down your ideas for specific market segments that may provide a good focus and how you can obtain names for your *Prospect Fishbowl.*

Robert E. Krumroy

Brand Positioning and Personality Are Imperative

The more specialized and distinct you can appear, the more attractive you become to your prospects. Lynn Upshaw, in *Building Brand Identity,* says, "simply building a brand identity fortress [name recognition] is not enough." He emphasizes that you must "create brand personality" to successfully attract the consumer. In other words, name recognition only does not create *brand positioning or brand personality,* both of which are necessary to create consumer attraction. Upshaw furthers this thought by saying, "When the strategic personality and positioning have been successfully blended, the result is a brand essence that is hard for prospects to

> *Service keeps clients. It doesn't attract new prospects. ...creating a local Identity Brand attracts new prospects.*

ignore." Name only does not drive the consumer to purchase your product or to want to meet with you. Neither will striving to perform your job better than the competition nor providing better service, though both are admirable goals. Service keeps clients. It doesn't attract new prospects. Building quality perception through creating a local *Identity Brand* attracts new prospects.

Without the brand components of positioning and personality, the argument that branding has occurred, particularly in a financial services industry, is hardly supportable unless the definition of branding is narrowed to being the company with the highest level of name recognition. That definition, however, is inappropriate. Branding is creating consumer attraction. Without that element, highly recognizable names such as Yugo and Edsel would be thriving brand products with consumer appeal. Obviously, they are not and neither is the sales professional who represents the insurance company or brokerage firm with the highest name recognition. Unless the representative creates *brand positioning* and *brand personality* locally, increasing the degree of your company's national

45

name recognition will provide little impact on your ability "to get in." The focus must turn to getting YOU to become distinctively different and unique. As your identity distinction increases locally, so does your initial consumer attraction. The degree of your local *Identity Brand* is what measures the level of your attractiveness to the consumer.

...increasing the degree of your company's national name recognition will provide little impact on your ability "to get in."

The degree of your local Identity Brand is what measures the level of your attractiveness...

How to Become Meaningfully Involved

The best networkers become involved with the group, give noticeable value, demonstrate appreciation for the organization and become uniquely visible. For instance, they may approach the board of directors of the city's recreational soccer league and offer to sponsor an appreciation night for the coaches, their market segment, by buying out an entire evening of a small local theater production and honoring them (the cost to do this is usually around $1,200). Consider cosponsoring this appreciation event with a wine merchant and include a free wine tasting during a thirty minute intermission. The wine merchant will provide the wine at cost or for free and would probably share the cost of the theater tickets. Obviously, you both would receive a lot of recognition for doing this and these people have now entered your *Prospect Fishbowl* for further familiarization over time.

Think about becoming involved with an organization and volunteering to help in fund-raising for their cause. For instance, you may have a real compassion for helping less financially fortunate people obtain home ownership and Habitat for Humanity would be a cause that could emotionally capture your interest. With your talent in sales, offer to help with corporate giving instead of, or in addition to, pounding nails. Become their number-one fundraiser! Not only will you feel good but also the group, as well as the business people from whom you solicit charitable contributions, will esteem you. There is no more honorable person than the person who does something to help someone else. Think of this same example with Hospice, The Childhood Leukemia Foundation or even your local college or university's athletic scholarship program. You didn't have to be graduated from there to recognize the value that a strong university adds to the quality of life in your town, so get involved and help raise money. If you become the best fundraiser, you will see the payoff in numerous ways. Be patient and consistent and save all of your contact names in your *Prospect Fishbowl.* You will continue to build a familiarization with these same prospects by continuing to provide valuable information over time.

Giving is the essence of high-performance networking. The *Bible,* says, "It is more blessed to give than to receive." If you *quit figuring out how to send a catchy solicitation letter...* want to attract favorable attention from your prospects, quit figuring out how to send a catchy solicitation letter (much less a multiple letter attack on colored paper) and start giving value to a group or organization that you care about. Build respect from within the group and you will get noticed, appreciated and eventually wealthy.

Build A Distinct and Unique Image

In order to become an effective networker you must learn *how to* develop "mindshare" within your individualized *Prospect Fishbowl.* Dan Kennedy, author of *The Ultimate Marketing Plan,* says, "Find your most promotable competitive edge, turn it into a powerful marketing message and deliver it to the right prospects." Dan is not referring to a general and nonindividualized target market. Neither is he referring to product features and benefits as your competitive edge. He is referring to individualizing your target market and promoting your personal distinction and uniqueness relative to the competition.

Most financial sales professionals think of print advertising when the word *promotion* is used. Don't! You must be more in the mind of the prospect than just a quality, knowledgeable professional who represents quality products and services, which is all that print advertising can convey. Those benefits alone are no longer adequate and neither does the prospect see them as distinctive. Furthermore, most sales professionals and companies view the world through product knowledge versus marketing knowledge. They believe that providing more advanced training for creating superior knowledge in product and service, relative to the competition, will increase prospect attraction. This is a faulty diagnosis of a marketing problem and an inaccurate conclusion.

Marketing is all about developing a preference that is based on your image. Image is built from being distinct and unique through providing experiences that constantly familiarize the prospect with you. It is not built by striving to become a better imitation of the competition. It is created by innovation and it doesn't have to be expensive. Author Dan Kennedy further says, "...entrepreneurs bankrupt themselves with expensive advertising and marketing schemes when their interest would be better served by low-cost methods." So, let's examine some low-cost methods for image building.

Image is built from being distinct and unique through providing experiences...

In order to begin creating a distinct and unique image you must first begin building an individualized *Prospect Fishbowl*. Choose a market segment(s), remember, no more than three and each one being sufficient in size (200+). If this group has a membership, make sure that you join once you are satisfied that the group is cohesive, large enough and can financially support your business focus. You will never be considered a colleague to a "membership group" unless you are a member. As part of your market segment(s), you may select a charitable organization where you can become highly recognized for your efforts in fundraising. Dr. Thomas Stanley, in *Networking With the Affluent,* says, "...affluent prospects see you at your best when you are helping others you volunteer for." So get involved. Get noticed. Be the best at the job and don't ever lose a name that you have encountered. Always build and continue to add to your *Prospect Fishbowl.*

What About Sending a Newsletter?

Once you have individualized your targeted market, you need to decide how to build and maintain a basic and consistent familiarization to the individuals about what you do. In other words, just because you go to the local homebuilders association each month, the Rotary meeting every week or even become the best fund-raiser for Urban Ministry, doesn't mean you have captured "mindshare" or preference in regard to your business. The author Dr. Thomas Stanley, says, "...the very best sellers and marketers offer clients much more than a core and often mundane product." What is it that you offer to capture

Consistent familiarization is the single most important element for building brand preference.

"mindshare"? I would suggest that you must consistently send an intellectual newsletter (not product hype or company information) not just to clients, which is a common mistake, but also to your entire *Prospect Fishbowl.* Consistent familiarization is the single most important element for building brand preference. There is no other alternative that provides the frequency of familiarization than that of a newsletter. A newsletter needs to be sent no less than eight times per year or it is a waste of time and money. A quarterly mailing is inadequate for creating preference. It has no chance of placing you foremost in the prospect's mind. When that can't occur, you can't become dominant.

Effective newsletters will always contain educational content about potential *problem issues* versus service or product solicitations. Additionally, if you want effective results, newsletters should always encourage the recipient to respond to the issue(s) being addressed. We call this "raise your hand" opportunities. Allow recipients opportunities to request more specific information when the subject attracts their interest. People do what they want to do when they want to do it. If you don't give them opportunities to express their interests, you both lose.

Provide for multiple ways of responding. Some clients won't respond if they need to call and request information. Some won't respond if they have to fill out a reply card. Others will only respond by email over the Internet, a percentage that our research indicates is over thirty percent of your market and rapidly growing. The conclusion is: Provide all three ways to respond and let your prospects choose one.

Another consideration is that a one-page newsletter has a better chance of being read than does a four-page one. Plus, they are a lot less expensive to purchase and mail. Don't believe the hype about a newsletter needing to be in color and on glossy paper. The *Kiplinger Washington Letter* is one of the most frequently read newsletters in the world. It is printed on cream paper with black ink, no color and contains no pictures. It underscores and bolds main points which make it

choosing between an expensive four-page newsletter sent quarterly or a newsletter being sent twice as often, eight times per year, choose the later.

easy for the recipient to scan. Frequency is far more important than length. If you are choosing between an expensive four-page newsletter sent quarterly or a newsletter being sent twice as often, eight times per year, choose the later. Consistent familiarization is the number-one component for building "mindshare" and the component that sales professionals most frequently compromise. Don't make this mistake.

If you believe that your national home office company correspondence, quarterly magazines, premium notices or annual reports make a "familiarization impact" on your clients and therefore helps to build you as the local brand, think again. These are not unique; some are not even pleasant experiences. Neither do they profile you. They are

*It is **your** local image that needs to be created as distinct and unique, not your company's.*

not helpful in capturing "mindshare." It is your local image that needs to be created as distinct and unique, not your company's.

Following are copies of two newsletters that give "value information" yet makes an effective appeal to the reader to request additional information.

$ *Money Impact*

A special newsletter for valued clients, friends and future clients

Volume III Issue 1

Compliments of...

Jeff Chambers, CLU, CFP
High Trust Life Insurance Co.
2007 Yanceyville Street, Suite 270
Greensboro, NC 27405

January 2000

Phone: 336-303-7316
FAX: 336-303-7318
Email: jeff@hightrust.com

TIME FLIES?   We all joke but life goes by pretty fast!

It's 10, 20, 30 years from now. **You're retired**. The phone rings. It's your 8-year-old **GRANDDAUGHTER** from "states away," USA. It's been six years now since your daughter and son-in-law moved because of their careers. **You smile** at the sound of your granddaughter's little voice every time she calls. You have a **SPECIAL BOND**. Her excitement for life is contagious. "Grandpa, Grandpa," her voice warms your heart, "I was **picked to play** Dorothy **in** our **school play**, THE WIZARD OF OZ. Can you believe it, Grandpa? You said that I should try out for the play. Well, I did and I GOT THE PART! Can you believe it? **You'll be so proud** of me, Grandpa. I want you to see me!"

Then the question comes, **"Will you and Grandma COME SEE ME?** You have to come see me in the play. Remember when we saw the movie together? **I'll hold your hand** and you can meet all of my friends. **PLEASE COME, Grandpa...Please?!"**

In that moment, frozen like eternity, the **pain swells** in your heart. You know that you and grandma visited in the spring and that your **retirement nest egg** just **won't allow you to go** again this year. **Retirement costs a lot more** than you imagined. No words are adequate for this moment and nothing can save the **LETDOWN** for your Granddaughter or the heaviness of your heart. "I'm so proud of you sweetheart, but Grandma and I just **CAN'T COME**. I really **wish** we could. Will you have your Mom take a **picture** and send it to us? I love you Sweetheart! We'll see you soon. OK?"

Are you **WAITING** until you make more money so you can save more? You're saving but **WONDER IF** you could be doing better. Do you **RISK MISSING** the plays someday, the **BEST MOMENTS** of your life! That's a **big price**. A preventable loss!

RETIREMENT GIVES NO SECOND CHANCES! Contact us for our **free information** package before year-end on "Retiring Comfortably." It might be the information that puts a **Granddaughter's hand in yours** while she takes you to **THE PLAY!**

(1215102001)

Robert E. Krumroy

Business Impact

Business Owners: "An Exclusive Focus. A Superior Expertise."

Volume III Issue 1

January 2000

Compliments of...

Laura McKinney, CLU, ChFC
High Trust Insurance Company
2007 Yanceyville Street, Suite 270
Greensboro, NC 27405

Phone: 336-303-7316
FAX: 336-303-7318
Email: Laura@hightrust.com

DREAMS DASHED.   A BUSINESS GONE.

Richard was 52 years old, a **BUSINESS OWNER** and happily married with two great children. His daughter, now 15 yrs old, would always be his 'little' girl. His son, now in his second year of college, was majoring in business. In two more years, his **son** would **join him as a business partner**. Watching him work over summer breaks with the business had been fulfilling but the **dream** he had imagined ever since the doctor had announced, "congratulations, it's a boy" was **close to becoming a reality**...OR **WOULD IT?**

Three months later, Richard phoned his son. The **PAIN in his heart**, frozen like eternity, felt like a dagger as he tried **to tell his son**. The words he spoke were more painful than the **cancer** that had surprised him and everyone else. His **DREAMS** were now **GONE!**

Dad died 2 years later. His *son* graduated and *took a job* with a corporate business. His *wife sold the business* for the inventory price of the equipment. The money, along with some life insurance death proceeds has gotten her and her daughter by, but **not like before**. Everyone's **dreams** have been **DASHED**. Everyone has paid a **price for poor planning**.

At some point, every business owner will EXIT his or her business. Most family businesses die with the owner. **Most die with inadequate planning**. Is being too busy really an excuse? Will it heal the heartache? When was the last time that you reviewed the latest **simple planning techniques** that the IRS allows for business owners? Tax laws change! **ARE YOU UP TO DATE?** There are **NO SECOND CHANCES** for your loved ones. The **futures** of your family members are in **your hands**.

Contact us by email, phone or reply form for our **FREE INFORMATION** packet on *Planning Options For Your Business*. **DON'T PUT IT OFF!** Do a **PRIVATE SELF EVALUATION** with this information. Too busy is a bad excuse. The PAIN you prevent will be FOREVER for someone. **CONTACT US NOW!** The information is **free**.
(121602001)

Creating Low Cost Unique Events and Finding Potential Market Allies

To become an Identity Brand within a specific market segment, your familiarization plan must favorably differentiate you from the competition. A perception of being unique and distinct must permeate your reputation. Conducting no less than four annual events per year to which you invite your *Prospect Fishbowl* will create a competitive advantage and start you well on your way to becoming the most recognizable and distinct professional within your market. Regis McKenna, author of *Real Time,* says, "Brand is more than a name. Brand is an active experience." The more creative you can be, the more distinctive your Identity Brand becomes. Even those who don't attend will take notice of the invitation and the uniqueness. Either way, the perception of appearing unique to the prospect has been accomplished. You are starting to build a local quality perception whose distinctiveness will eventually become your brand.

Regis McKenna, author of Real Time, says, "Brand is more than a name. Brand is an active experience."

To appear unique, to reduce cost and to attract new prospects to your events, consider allying yourself with someone who desires the same type of exposure to similar types of prospects. For instance, invite a psychologist to conduct a yearly event on "How to Help Students With Learning Disabilities Choose a College and Complete Their Degrees." You can send a letter inviting any parent of school age children to attend. The presentation is shared as well as the cost, which should be minimal if the event is held in a library, college, etc. Another example is to become known for conducting an annual event at the beginning of every new year such as, "The Best Investments and Best All-Inclusive Vacations For the New Year – An Evening of Fun." Not only could a local travel agency share the cost but you could also ask a new catering company to participate by providing hors d'oeuvres at cost. Invite them both to contribute their client lists for the mailing. This is a great promotion for you and it benefits the travel and catering companies as well. Your prospects are the same prospects they want to influence.

Now that your creative mind is working, how about "A Taste of Wine for the Autumn Times – An Evening of Wine Tasting and Investment Tips"? Guess who provides the wine FOR FREE! Want to do a spring theme? Invite your best forty clients to an annual client appreciation night called, "Croquet and Chardonnay – Please Wear Your English Whites for an Evening of Merriment." Mention in the invitation that this is a "Friends Bringing Friends" event. Your *Prospect Fishbowl* will be the recipient of numerous new prospects whom will be impressed with your uniqueness relative to the competition.

> *Invite your best forty clients to an annual client appreciation night called, "Croquet and Chardonnay–Please Wear Your English Whites for an Evening of Merriment."*

If you're a financial advisor attempting to build your brand presence, as well as add qualified family names to your *Prospect Fishbowl,* here is a unique idea, but only if the commonality is genuine. Get a local theater to allow you to purchase an entire mid-morning showing (approximately $300-$500) of an appropriate movie for children such as *The Prince of Egypt.* Align yourself with the leading Christian bookstore in your area. Promote the event with a mailer, which you produce, and with additional flyers to be handed out at the bookstore's cash register. Both should include the message that you and the bookseller both appreciate the customer's patronage of the bookstore. The free children's tickets are available at the bookstore for clients and customers who come into the store to register. Plan for a three-hour event and contact the local YMCA or a church junior high youth group about providing teenage chaperones (usually free or for a very small donation). Give away helium balloons; hold drawings for children's prizes, a twenty-five dollar gift certificate from the bookstore and four tickets to the theater, which will be donated. Use the forms the parents fill out to register their children for the free movie as the entry forms for the drawings. Make sure that the form includes the parent's name, address, phone number and email address. Remember, these new people go into your *Prospect Fishbowl* for further familiarization over time.

The next few pages contain a few examples of invitations inviting prospects and clients to unique events that demonstrate aligning yourself with market allies.

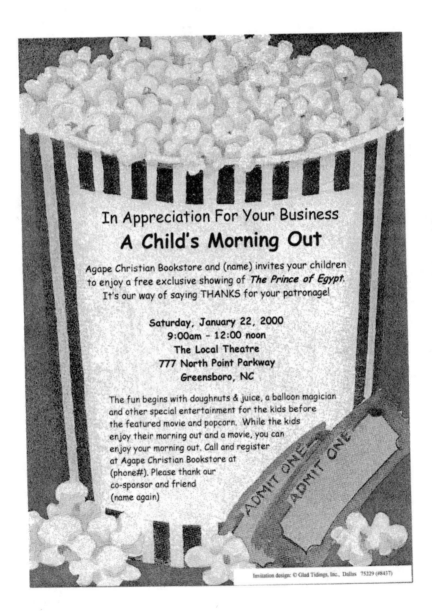

In Appreciation For Your Business
A Child's Morning Out

Agape Christian Bookstore and (name) invites your children to enjoy a free exclusive showing of *The Prince of Egypt*. It's our way of saying THANKS for your patronage!

Saturday, January 22, 2000
9:00am – 12:00 noon
The Local Theatre
777 North Point Parkway
Greensboro, NC

The fun begins with doughnuts & juice, a balloon magician and other special entertainment for the kids before the featured movie and popcorn. While the kids enjoy their morning out and a movie, you can enjoy your morning out. Call and register at Agape Christian Bookstore at (phone#). Please thank our co-sponsor and friend (name again)

Invitation design: © Glad Tidings, Inc., Dallas 75329 (#8437)

Viva Italia!

AN ANNUAL CLIENT APPRECIATION NIGHT
Friends Bringing Friends

Agent X and High Trust Insurance Company cordially invite you to enjoy an unforgettable evening at our Annual Client Appreciation Italian Festival. Spend an evening with other clients, plus bring your friends, and indulge yourself with fabulous Italian food along with an Italian wine tasting and dancing. Enjoy an intriguing presentation during dinner on *Italy – How to go and what to see*, presented by (travel group) and a 12-minute presentation on *12-Month Economic Forecast and Investment Predictions.* Now, bring out the band...Let's dance the evening away! Don't miss this event!

Saturday, January 15, 2000
7:00 pm – 11:00 pm
Country Club, City

Reservations are needed. Space is limited so *RSVP* early by contacting (name) at 336-303-7316.

Invitation design: © Four Seasons Publishing, Inc. Portland, ME (No. I-211)

Recreating Traditional Events to Attract More Attendees

The birth of any brand is always initiated with an experience that impacts the prospect. The establishment of brand preference, within the consumers mind, is the culmination of multiple experiences and consistent familiarization. There is a tremendous benefit in consistently conducting periodic traditional events, such as bringing in mutual fund managers in order to continually impact your individualized market segment(s). You can increase attendance, as well as your distinctiveness, by stamping them with your personal touch by being creative in naming these events.

Instead of simply inviting prospects and clients to quarterly investment seminars, briefs or workshops, all of which have been overdone, invite them to "events" and give them more intriguing titles such as, *"Predictions Revealed* for Attaining *'Home Run'* Investment Returns Over the Next Five Years."* Doesn't that title sound more interesting than "Opportunities in Value Investing"? How about, "The Newest *Secrets* for *Maximizing Returns* [including your 401(k) account], *Minimizing Risk* and *'Smashing Those Taxes'* "or *"Securing Large Profits* While *Avoiding Deep Losses!* The Stock Market Will Make a *Correction.* "These titles are much more appealing, distinctive and memorable than, "Stock Market Trends and Opportunities" or "Tax Smart Investing." Try to use words that elicit emotion, attract curiosity and imply that you may have information that your prospects and clients would like to have; words such as, *"secrets,"* *"predictions,"* "avoid,*"or *'revealing"* are intriguing and difficult words to ignore. Here is one final example: "The *'Newest'* Investment Secrets* that You *Must Know* for Attaining *Superior Returns.* "Creative titles will draw more attraction and help in creating your Identity Brand of being distinct, unique and differentiated relative to the competition.

Usually the broker dealer will assume most of the cost for these events. You just need to get the attendees there. If you have your *Prospect Fishbowl* built, that will be easy. Imagine the impact on your prospects as they continually get invited to both consistent and unique events and receive consistent intellectual communications from you. Remember, any of these events can be promoted as "Friends Bringing Friends."

Write down some ideas for your consistent events that would help Identity Brand your distinction within your market segment.

Get Published in a Trade Journal or Newsletter

What else can you do? How about writing an article for publication in your group association's newsletter or trade journal? Just call the publications editors and ask. They will treat you like a gift from heaven. The article could be on risk management, investing or tax reduction strategies, but it could also be something creative such as "Why The New Marketing Revolution Will Change Your Company's Marketing Strategy" or "What Consumers Want...It's More Than Your Core Product or Service." You might create an article on "Effective Selling Methods to Increase Sales" by applying your selling system to their type of product or service. Topics that offer clients information to enhance their income are appreciated far more than self-promotion. Whatever your topic, the tagline at the end of the article always identifies you to the audience as the contributing author. Be sure that you make reprints and send them to the people in your *Prospect Fishbowl* that you want to influence. Keep a stack of reprints for future use. Getting published in their trade journal or local newsletter is a great way to validate your expertise to your prospect. However, don't assume that everyone saw or will remember your article. Feel free to give them a little help. Promote your accomplishment.

List opportunities and topic ideas for writing an article.

Don't Golf in a Sponsored Golf Tournament

Another inexpensive promotion strategy with a group with which you are already involved is to help sponsor their golf tournament. DO NOT sign up to play golf with a foursome! Instead, ask to sponsor one of the "watering holes" where beer and soft drinks are given to the golfers. Sponsorship of a hole will usually cost between one hundred to two hundred dollars. Get a lawn chair and wait to greet each foursome as they make the rounds. Hand out the beer and soft drinks, but also bring along a quantity of

Do NOT sign up to play golf with a foursome!

cigars, both tobacco and bubble gum so that no one feels left out. Get the one-dollar golf specials. Any cigar shop can help you out. The golfers will remember you as the cigar person!

Have a camera handy and take a picture of every foursome. Have four prints made of each group. At the end of the event, offer to send a thank-you letter to each golfer that expresses appreciation for their participating in the fund-raiser, announces the financial results of the event and includes a picture of them with their golfing buddies. You will want to hand-deliver some of these, particularly to the golfers that asked questions about you and seemed interested in your opinion on financial issues. Participating in a golf tournament, in this manner, is unique and you will get many favorable comments. The fund-raising committee will think you are a genius. You can easily get a roster of foursomes in the order that they will arrive at your hole. You will know their names except for the last-minute substitutions and you can verify all names, company affiliations and addresses as you take their picture. Except for your financial service competitor, who came past your hole with the three clients that he invited to play, put everyone else into your *Prospect Fishbowl.*

Cigar Aficionados

You may want to make a special note of the serious cigar smokers when sponsoring your golf tournament. In the future, when you organize a cigar-dinner event, co-sponsored with a cigar store (they will supply free cigars), a wine merchant (free wine)and a new caterer (food at cost and split three ways), these are great people to include on the invitation list. The format for this event opens with thirty minutes of hors d'oeuvres. Invite the guests to be seated at rectangular tables arranged at forty-five degree angles so that everyone can see the front of the room (don't use round tables). Begin the evening with a fifteen-minute presentation introducing the first cigar. Follow this with a ten-minute presentation introducing the first wine and then complete this first segment with a ten to twelve-minute presentation on investment strategies. Invite a mutual fund manager to be present and they will normally pay for all or part of the food cost. Break for a forty-five minute pasta bar extravaganza. Reconvene for the second segment in which the order of presentations is reversed: investments (twelve minutes), wine (ten minutes) and a final cigar presentation (fifteen minutes). Place evaluation forms at the tables during the pasta course for collection at the end. Announce that a drawing for a few bottles of wine, another one for six fine cigars and a final one for a free copy of a best selling business or financial book such as *The Millionaire Next Door,* by Dr. Thomas Stanley will be conducted at the end of the final cigar presentation-so please complete and be ready to hand in the evaluation at the end. You may choose to add dessert or coffee, but it is not necessary. The total cost incurred for this event should be inclusive of food (consisting of the pasta bar and hors d'oeuvres) and possible room rental. If one hundred people attended and the costs were split between the three sponsors, each person's expenditure could be kept to under five hundred dollars and the mutual fund manager may pick up your share.

Other than the cigar smokers that you know, whom do you invite? Just ask the cigar merchant, the wine merchant and the food caterer

A purchased list from a list broker will produce a disappointment.

for lists of their best clients. They all want to create deeper "mindshare" and they too need to appear unique to their clients. They will love the creativeness of your idea. Our experience is that you will get at least ten to twelve percent of the invitees to attend. A list of seven hundred will produce seventy to eighty attendees. Don't buy cigar smoker names from a list broker. These people come because of relationships with the sponsors. A purchased list from a list broker will produce a disappointment. The sponsors have their own lists and they will participate. Oh...and don't forget where all the names go...into your *Prospect Fishbowl*.

Our first cigar dinner attracted eighty-three attendees; thirty percent of the group was female. Only five of the attendees were past clients. The remaining attendees were people from the lists provided by the cigar and wine merchant. At the end of the evening, the evaluation forms indicated that over thirty attendees wanted to be contacted for the purpose of discussing financial issues pertaining specifically to them. Within six weeks, profits from new business exceeded total costs by over ten fold. The wine and cigar merchant were equally pleased with their results and wanted to repeat the event. If you are a cigar aficionado, you should repeat this event quarterly. Many attendees will return. People come back to "EVENTS." Events are fun! They are unlikely to come back to "SEMINARS." So here is a tip: Start calling your functions and seminars "events." Make them fun and watch them become popular and well attended. Even you will enjoy yourself more.

Events are fun!

Start calling your functions and seminars "events."

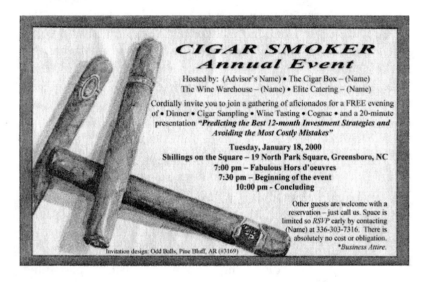

CIGAR SMOKER
Annual Event

Hosted by: (Advisor's Name) • The Cigar Box – (Name)
The Wine Warehouse – (Name) • Elite Catering – (Name)

Cordially invite you to join a gathering of aficionados for a FREE evening
of • Dinner • Cigar Sampling • Wine Tasting • Cognac • and a 20-minute
presentation *"Predicting the Best 12-month Investment Strategies and
Avoiding the Most Costly Mistakes"*

Tuesday, January 18, 2000
Shillings on the Square – 19 North Park Square, Greensboro, NC
7:00 pm – Fabulous Hors d'oeuvres
7:30 pm – Beginning of the event
10:00 pm - Concluding

Other guests are welcome with a
reservation – just call us. Space is
limited so *RSVP* early by contacting
(Name) at 336-303-7316. There is
absolutely no cost or obligation.
Business Attire.

Invitation design: Odd Balls, Pine Bluff, AR (#3169)

Cigar Smoker Dinner

Sample Agenda:

7:00 p.m.	Opening hors d'oeuvres	30 minutes
7:30	General Welcome	5 minutes
7:35	1st Cigar Introduction	15 minutes
7:50	1st Wine Presentation	10 minutes
8:00	1st Investment Strategy	12 minutes
8:12	PASTA BAR	45 minutes
	(Place evaluation forms at each table)	
9:00	Re-welcome – explain evaluation	
	form and end of evening drawings	3 minutes
9:03	2nd Investment Strategy	12 minutes
9:15	2nd Wine Presentation	10 minutes
9:25	2nd Cigar Presentation	15 minutes
9:40	Free Drawings	10 minutes
	(Collect evaluation forms)	
9:50	Conclusion – dessert and coffee optional	

Drawings:
1) 2 Bottles of wine
2) 4-6 Cigars
3) A book such as *The Millionaire Next Door,* by Dr. Thomas Stanley or *The Roaring 2000's,* by Harry Dent.

• Wine and cigars should be provided for free.

• Food should be split 3 ways. The caterer may provide it at cost.

• All attendee names should be given to all presenters, including the caterer, for their database.

• The reverse order of investment presentations and cigar presentations during the second part of the event will keep the attendees attentive and prevent early departures.

Should You Participate in Trade Shows?

Do any of your market segment groups have statewide annual trade shows? Consider participating (particularly if you have been published in their trade journal or newsletter), but instead of purchasing a booth to hand out boring company brochures and literature, ask to sponsor the coffee booth, at a cost usually no more

Company brochures don't help!

than two hundred dollars. Hand out coffee in paper cups with your or your company's name printed on them, and concentrate on greeting, meeting and making the attendees feel welcomed. Be an ambassador for the organization. Get to know the people. Ask how the conference is going. Ask if you can assist with any of their needs. Announce that you are giving out candy bars at the breaks. A Snicker's or a Milky Way is received with a lot more enthusiasm than a Roth IRA brochure! Get a list of attendees from the organization and note the "friendly folks" as you talk with them. Keep a notepad to remember these special people. Your objective is to become popular and appreciated. Company brochures don't help!

If you are helping to sponsor their golf tournament the day before the conference or trade show begins, don't forget to take pictures of each golfing foursome as was mentioned earlier. However, since you are going to be in the exhibition hall, preferably at the coffee booth, consider videotaping each of their golf drives. Don't hire this to be done. The amateur approach is much funnier and the personal contacts you are making is the significant point. You might have an assistant travel around in a golf cart taking cameo videos of sand trap shots, their putting expertise and the fabulous chipping talent that gets displayed. Play this video on a TV behind the coffee booth. Trust me! You will not only attract the attendees, but the other exhibitors will wonder why they have no traffic and why everyone is staying at the coffee booth. Any other financial participant will cringe at the printed coffee cups. They know that they just got beat out in regard to making an impression. You have just witnessed consumer preference being formed, "mindshare" being captured! You are offering more than your core product and service. It will pay off handsomely.

What market segment conferences or trade shows can you participate in?

Give Your VIPs Special Attention

Instead of sending your top twenty-five to forty clients birthday cards, identify these people as your VIP list and personally deliver a birthday cake to each of their offices. You can just drop by, or call the secretary first if you want to make sure that the VIP is there. This gesture and birthday recognition is cheaper

identify…your VIP list and personally deliver a birthday cake to each of their offices.

than lunch and it has never happened to them. Never! Make your visit around 11:00 a.m. and watch who gets invited to lunch and who will insist on paying. The whole point is to look unique and distinctly different than the normal competition. Creating a superior *value perception* will require applying uniqueness and innovation. If you can look unique, not only will the business come your way but so will the referrals. You won't have to coerce the prospect for them either.

What About CPA Referrals?

The question is always asked, "What about CPAs? I understand that they can be a great source of endorsements." Many CPA firms will eventually evaluate whether it is to their and their client's best advantage to create a financial service company alliance in order to offer financial planning. For CPA firms interested in sharing commissions or fees, the driving motivation is profits. Their choice as to whom they will develop this relationship with is important, but the final selection will be determined primarily on the thoroughness of the business proposal and their perception of competency. They will choose someone or some firm based on qualifications and not on friendship.

The CPA who desires a compensatory alliance will use a selection criterion that will differ from the CPA who does not want a compensatory arrangement. The most appealing compensatory arrangement for a CPA will provide complete details regarding all phases of the working relationship, samples of financial plans designed for clients, detailed profit projections and detailed explanations as to how you will support their new SEC compliance and supervisory roles. *Compliance* to a CPA is not a bad word. It is a comforting word. A CPAs job includes keeping their clients out of trouble. If you emphasize your support of compliance and offer to either handle or meaningfully assist in their new compliance supervisory responsibilities, you will gain a significant advantage over the competition that does not address it. Whether the CPA firm wants a compensatory or noncompensatory relationship, they all want proof of competency, objectivity and trust. Unless you have visibly established your local reputation and up-to-date capability by conducting local CPA continuing education courses, which almost anyone can register and conduct with a submitted outline to your state's CPA board, convincing a CPA firm that you should develop a formal shared client relationship will be difficult. A national company that will support these arrangements, assist the financial advisor with a thoroughly defined national program and include legal agreements, which must be signed by both parties, will create a perception of depth and safety that will have an even greater appeal to the CPA firm. In summary: Detailed formal structure, compliance assistance and legal agreements coupled with proven capabilities will be a winning combination. Now, let's address the CPA who wants to maintain the "purity of his or her profession" by keeping a taxation focus only, which many will choose as an option.

According to Russ Prince and Karen File, authors of the book *Marketing Through Advisors,* "36% of accountants made referrals of affluent clients to life insurance professionals in the last year." However, there is a catch. In order for you to effectively position yourself to win over advisors, you will need to become an expert at creating among these advisors an awareness about yourself, your practice and the services you provide. According to Prince and File in their interviews with CPAs, most agents make the mistake of looking for a handout every time they are with their CPA (90.8%). CPAs are unanimously unappreciative of this (0.0%) and they do not regard it as an effective way to build the relationship. The goal should be to provide value, which could be

most agents make the mistake of looking for a handout every time they are with their CPA

enhanced by regularly sending financial articles of interest. Display your expertise by giving quarterly CE seminars either at their firm or at colleges or libraries. Publish a yearly schedule of quarterly CE seminars one year in advance, which builds confidence in the depth of your expertise. Continually maintain constant familiarization by providing a frequently published technical newsletter (many are available) and then meet with them, at least quarterly, to ask how you can help with **their needs**. Finally, become friends. Find a CPA that you genuinely like and start the process. Be patient and don't ask for referrals. Advisors are well aware that you would appreciate leads. When the time comes, if you have captured the "mindshare," you will be rewarded often. Just remember, this is a long-term project. Be consistent in maintaining contact and patient in giving the process adequate time to yield results.

What CPA firm should I contact and begin cultivating a relationship with?

What About a Property & Casualty Alliance?

An alliance between a property and casualty firm and a life insurance professional, or a financial advisor, is potentially one of the most profitable alliances that either party can form. However, it is also one of the hardest alliances to achieve due to the perception of differences in goals and objectives of each organization. Unless those perceptions can be addressed up front, the success of putting together an alliance, much less making one last, will be limited or completely lacking.

Before addressing the challenges and how to overcome them, both parties together should review the benefits of an alliance and decide if they are complementary to their business goals. There are four major benefits for creating an alliance that are worthy of consideration.

Four Benefits of Creating a Successful Property & Casualty Alliance

1. An alliance can help both organizations spread or avoid costs while providing a new business channel for increasing profits.

2. P&C companies gain an enhanced respect from their customers if they promote that they are extending a new service by forming a link with a specialist. It implies that they are maintaining a narrow focus to maintain a higher level of expertise in their field than their competitors. They are also acknowledging that they are addressing their customers' additional needs with an equally higher level of expertise than an "all service" organization would be capable of providing. This "endorsement" of sorts increases the customers' perception of specialized expertise and high level of client concern.

3. Each party gains an immediate credibility with those customers that they share when needs arise. Trust is passed on and, therefore, must be honored as "an entrusted gift to be handled with the utmost respect by the recipient."

4. Creating a deeper client loyalty through alliance marketing will help insulate the client from competitors, as well as direct-selling attempts from competing companies in the new technology age of marketing. The more commodity-like your product is, the easier it becomes to "price shop." P&C coverage is an easier target for direct-marketing attacks than a creative split-dollar executive benefit plan is. However, unless the parties create an emotional bond with the client, the client remains vulnerable to outside direct database marketing pursuits.

Roman G Hiebing Jr. and Scott W. Cooper, authors of *The One-Day Marketing Plan,* say, "It is harder for competitors to attack emotional relationships than specific product attributes once a relationship is established." Additionally, most consumers are less concerned about "better and best" in today's world of product proliferation and far more concerned with keeping things simple. That is why brands, according to Harry Beckwith, author of *Selling the Invisible,* account for ninety-three percent of all products purchased by consumers. Brands offer a perception of safety. Within today's society of information overload, we are less concerned about our *brand choice* being the best, whether choosing a consumable product or a service professional, than we are about insulating ourselves from new information that challenges our past conclusions. Insulating ourselves from challenging information allows us to simplify our lives. Kevin J. Clancy and Robert S. Shulman, authors of *Marketing Myths That Are Killing Business* agree: "Consumers no longer feel the need to buy the "best"...products; they are saying that there are better things to do with their time and money." In doing their research, they found that the majority of consumers agreed with the statement, "I don't have time to investigate the quality of different brands..." All of this supports the conclusion that, once a strong relationship bond is formed with a client, the relationship will withstand most product challenges.

in the market place today...it is imperative that an emotional bond with your client be formed and continually nurtured.

With the array of product choices in the market place today and the constant onslaught of marketing attacks, it is imperative that an emotional bond with your client be formed and continually nurtured. Bonded relationships begin with a personal experience and are maintained in the same way. The more frequent the contact, the more solid the bond. When a strategic alliance is successful, the perceived depth of expertise is enhanced and the contact frequency is increased, all of which creates a deeper commitment to the chosen brand. Everyone wins, but most important, the client benefits.

With all the benefits available to both parties from structuring an alliance, why does it seem so difficult to initiate and maintain it? There are four major obstacles that must be overcome.

Four Property & Casualty Alliance Obstacles That Must Be Overcome

1. Perceived loss of control by the P&C firm

2. Fear of losing a client due to the other party's behavior

3. Being represented by someone who does not share the same value for their client base that they spent years to build

4. Poor communication

All of these obstacles can be resolved if both parties will take the time to openly discuss their concerns. Usually, the greatest fears are on the P&C side and rightfully so. The majority of their income is renewal income in contrast to the life agent's first-year commission stream. Regardless of the life agent's sincere insistence that he or she values their clients, the compensation difference is a troublesome issue for the P&C firm. It can cause an easy jump to the conclusion that sales, and not service, are the number-one concern. That is the first roadblock that must be circumvented. Acknowledge the fact that you will never resolve this issue in the beginning with one hundred percent comfort. It will only resolve itself over time as both parties view the actions of each other. However, there are some steps that can be taken to add some degree of comfort for the P&C firm.

Most P&C firms are going to be resistant to opening their entire files to the life agent without any control. On the other hand, it is unrealistic for the P&C firm to think that the client will somehow contact them when he or she is ready for a buy-sell, a deferred compensation plan, an age-weighted profit-sharing plan or even a simple mutual fund or a financial plan. It simply won't happen. What can happen is that

you can jointly send a systematic communication, a joint newsletter, to the client...

you can jointly send a systematic communication, a joint newsletter, to the client that provides educational information, not product solicitation, on a regular basis. This communication must give the client the ability to easily respond when they want more details. A reply card or the ability to send an email response is a must. This same database of clients should also be invited to attend periodic and unique events. Build an Identity Brand together as a team. Develop a plan and stick to it. Once the relationship starts to take hold, the P&C firm will become more receptive to discussing clients that they feel should be proactively contacted. Give it time.

If you do a regular educational-type mailing (which to be effective should go out at least eight times per year), allow the client responses to go directly back to the P&C firm. Remember, one of the largest roadblocks was control. The P&C firm can then review them and decide how much control they want to maintain when the contact is made, such as requesting that a meeting be scheduled jointly or that it be held in their office. The life insurance agent, or financial advisor, needs to be responsible for the educational newsletter mailing, but the control of replies and the initial contact decision should be offered to the P&C firm. Once this relationship develops, you will see increasing cooperation. The P&C firm will delegate more and more authority as their confidence builds that you have their best interest at heart and not your own pocketbook.

A further word of caution: Ask the P&C firm if they want the client mailing to show the agent's or financial advisor's name or if they prefer to simply indicate that a strategic alliance with a "business market center" or an "estate specialist" has been formed. Arguing about putting the sales professional's name on the client mailing can stop an alliance discussion almost immediately. The sales professional's job in the relationship should be viewed as helping to develop the "Brand" reputation of the P&C firm, not their own. The sales professional should be focused on giving additional value recognition to the P&C firm's special needs as an enhancement to the P&C firm's reputation, rather than as a way to "get" more clients. That will happen as a result of focusing on "giving," instead of focusing on "getting." If you help the P&C firm get what they want, they will eventually help you get more than you ever expected. Building a solid relationship with a P&C firm is like maintaining a good marriage. Once you have initiated the discussion about forming an alliance, don't let it be you who gives them a reason to leave.

> *The sales professional's job...helping to develop the "Brand" reputation of the P&C firm, not their own.*

What P&C firm should I approach about an alliance/branding relationship?

Business Impact

Business Owners: "An Exclusive Focus. A Superior Expertise."

Volume III Issue 1   **A Professional Service Alliance**   January 2000

Laura McKinney, CLU, ChFC
High Trust Insurance Company
2007 Yanceyville Street, Suite 270
Greensboro, NC 27405
Phone: 336-303-7316
FAX: 336-303-7318
Email: laura@hightrust.com

Mary Grant, Agent
P & C Company USA
555 Main Street
Greensboro, NC 27555
Phone: 555-934-1203
FAX: 555-934-8713
Email: mary@p&ccompanyusa.com

DREAMS DASHED. A BUSINESS GONE.

Richard was 52 years old, a **BUSINESS OWNER** and happily married with two great children. His daughter, now 15 yrs old, would always be his 'little' girl. His son, now in his second year of college, was majoring in business. In two more years, his **son** would **join him as a business partner**. Watching him work over summer breaks with the business had been fulfilling but the **dream** he had imagined ever since the doctor had announced, "congratulations, it's a boy" was **close to becoming a reality**...OR **WOULD IT?**

Three months later, Richard phoned his son. The **PAIN in his heart**, frozen like eternity, felt like a dagger as he tried **to tell his son.** The words he spoke were more painful than the **cancer** that had surprised him and everyone else. His **DREAMS** were now **GONE!**

Dad died 2 years later. His *son* graduated and *took a job* with a corporate business. His *wife sold the business* for the inventory price of the equipment. The money, along with some life insurance death proceeds has gotten her and her daughter by, but **not like before**. Everyone's **dreams** have been **DASHED**. Everyone has paid a **price for poor planning**.

At some point, every business owner will EXIT his or her business. Most family businesses die with the owner. **Most die with inadequate planning.** Is being too busy really an excuse? Will it heal the heartache? When was the last time that you reviewed the latest **simple planning techniques** that the IRS allows for business owners? Tax laws change! **ARE YOU UP TO DATE?** There are **NO SECOND CHANCES** for your loved ones. The **futures** of your family members are in **your hands.**

Contact us by email, phone or reply form for our **FREE INFORMATION** packet on *Planning Options For Your Business.* **DON'T PUT IT OFF!** Do a **PRIVATE SELF EVALUATION** with this information. Too busy is a bad excuse. The PAIN you prevent will be FOREVER for someone. **CONTACT US NOW!** The information is **free.**
(121602001)

Don't Confuse Target Selling With Target Marketing

Many sales professionals and managers confuse target selling with target marketing. Not only are the two distinctly different, but eventually their paths will take you to two different destinations. Target marketing, when done correctly, allows you to become Identity Branded within an emotionally cohesive group of people who have the financial means to complement your

Identity Branding "who you are"...creates consumer pull...attraction

talent capability. In other words, if your talent capability allows you to apply your skill level to the sophisticated executive compensation market, you would eventually become highly discouraged if your daily routine was working with young married couples. Even if you could increase your income, you would eventually become dissatisfied and bored because you would be underemployed. Your skill level would be underutilized. Marketing, by individualizing your *Prospect Fishbowl,* allows you to evolve your prospects upward by adding some and eliminating others over time. Furthermore, Identity Branding "who you are" to your prospects, creates consumer pull. Ultimately, it creates an attraction where the consumer not only accepts your request for an appointment but actually wants to meet with you.

Conversely, an example of target selling may be getting yourself in front of a group of people who have little commonality but somehow got placed together in a meeting or seminar. You may have convinced a large employer to allow you to do a series of seminars for their employees. They may have even approved a payroll deduction option for their employees. If this is your intended business strategy, fine. If not, you may meet your sales or commission goal but the majority of your sales will more than likely not utilize your talents. As your educational development continues, you may eventually feel trapped within a nonchallenging market. You will realize that not only do you have limited access to the higher income markets that you are capable of handling, but you have no "mindshare" of the prospects you desire to contact. Your focus has been directed elsewhere. This is the unfortunate result and final destination of building one's business from a selling model, versus a marketing model.

Another example of target selling, versus target marketing, is the sales professional who calls on newly married couples, new mortgage leads, new births, newly retired people and even newly formed businesses (with no other identifying characteristic). You may get some sales, but the market characteristics of commonality, frequent communication and shared purpose between the individuals, which make up the definition of a market segment, are probably nonexistent. If this is an initial effort to accumulate potential prospects for familiarization within your *Prospect Fishbowl,* which later can be sorted out to fit your talent level, your efforts may serve a valuable purpose (depending on the amount of time this strategy takes). There is nothing wrong with introducing new prospects to your *Prospect Fishbowl* that initially add intrigue, even if you are not sure that they initially fit. If the cultivation cost and time to acquire these names is hardly noticeable, you may end up pleasantly surprised, but immediately discard names that you find do not match your prospect profile or your talent level. If your efforts at target selling to a loosely defined market, even if through seminars, are just to drive sales results from any breathing prospect, eventually you will stop regardless of your commission success. You will find no sustaining career fulfillment. You will quit, go to a different company, or become motivationally stalled and reach a production plateau.

A marketing focus builds your future. A target selling focus may provide immediate income, but it will not provide the motivation to stay the course. Neither will you feel any more secure three years from now in this business. You will still be wondering where your next sale will come from. You will know that you have captured no "mindshare" within any particular prospect market and you will be keenly aware that you have no unique prospect attraction relative to the competition.

Marketing is not just something you do to get into the door; it determines the long-term satisfaction that you will derive from your efforts. It is what sustains the personal feelings of accomplishment. The sales professionals who build

sales professionals...who build their business from a marketing platform, versus a selling platform...are generously rewarded.

their business from a marketing platform, versus a selling platform, will find a prospect community that will appreciate them, acknowledge their character and generously reward them with their business. You will be regarded as one who gives generously of themselves, and the prospect community will generously give back.

Markets to Avoid

A word of caution may help you avoid focusing your marketing efforts on organizations that will eventually prove to be disappointing. Don't focus your marketing efforts on non-cohesive organizations that people join because others "expect them to join" or to groups that they might be members of for only a short period of time, i.e., the Better Business Bureau, your child's school PTA. Some of these organizations may be cohesive, particularly in smaller towns, and may prove to be good choices, but others are so large that being a member may be expected, but your membership carries no weight when influencing someone to do business with you. This is not a commentary on the value or importance of these groups. Many of these organizations play a vital role within your community and should be supported with your membership dollars. However, a group that you will want to choose as a market segment focus must have members who want to sincerely be affiliated, want to contribute to the cause and the cause must have a lasting place in their hearts. Just ask yourself if most members would want to attend an adult-only holiday social, hosted by the group. If not, you have limited cohesiveness. The board of directors and officers may be cohesive, but that is not adequate for making an impact on the market segment if the majority of the group is emotionally uninvolved. Doing business with one member will have no influence on another member's opinion of you. In other words, you will be unable to create market preference within this group.

Some Other "Don'ts!"

Are there things that you shouldn't do, things that will probably just be a waste of money and time? Yes! Don't purchase space in a community tradeshow, i.e., the city's annual business expo, the home living show, the Christmas/holiday show. Remember, we are focusing on building our business on a marketing model, not a selling model.

build a prospect highway that continuously provides welcomed access to a prospect community and utilizes your skill level...

We want to build a prospect highway that continuously provides welcomed access to a prospect community and utilizes your skill level, not just do things for making another sale. If your group is noncohesive and weakly defined, your efforts will not help create a specific market segment that provides a prospect highway to prospects with consumer attraction. As Dan Kennedy says in *The Ultimate Marketing Plan*,"...every business ...appeals much more strongly to a certain definable group of people than it appeals to all people." If you attempt to appeal to everyone, you will appeal to no one. You probably won't even appeal to YOURSELF.

A community trade show attracts a group of people that is too general. The show's theme of fishing, home improvement or boats has nothing in common with the typical financial advisor. The cellular phone exhibition booth, though not what the attendees came to see, may attract some interest because cellular phones are a commodity and are used daily by a lot of people. But no one is carrying around his or her insurance policy or investment portfolio in hopes that someone will be around to answer a pressing financial question. In addition, attendees share no characteristic commonality and represent no specific market segment. The only commonality is that the general trade show attendees plus you will both be irritated and disappointed that you participated. That is not a good basis for starting a relationship.

Don't include an insurance solicitation to your clients due to their age increase with a birthday card or within a birthday letter. Believe it or not, the word is out. They know that the letter is intended to get new business much more than to convey a sincere birthday wish. If you want to send birthday wishes, leave the business stuff out!

Don't purchase a general prospect list from a list broker to get your *Prospect Fishbowl* project underway. The only exception (which I think is questionable) is the sales professional that intentionally works from a selling model due to a singular product focus, not a marketing model, and does not want, need or desire a lasting client relationship. This person normally sells a single product to a narrow audience that is usually purchased only once in their lifetime, i.e., long-term care insurance, Medicare supplement insurance, indexed annuities to prospects over age seventy. Buying a list is a lazy alternative to finding markets. There will be no cohesiveness in this group, if you can call it a group, and there is nothing that will provide an emotional pull to capture your interest or theirs. The incubation period

> *Don't purchase a general prospect list from a list broker to get your Prospect Fishbowl project underway.*

from a purchased list will be at least three to five years, if ever, to produce the same results that you could get in six months. A purchased list will prove disastrous for putting together a lasting market that provides continued growth and personal satisfaction.

Endorsements or Referrals?...Both!

Building an effective prospect foundation, a *Prospect Fishbowl*, is the culmination of identifying a market segment(s) and then individualizing the prospects so that you can create a favorable impact in order to create preference, a superior value perception and a competitive advantage. If you don't obtain and know the individual names of your prospects, this would be an impossible task. Your objective is to eventually "own" the market segment, not just a "market share." The ultimate goal is to create a perception of distinction and differentiation, to become the professional of choice to an identified market.

While you are identifying your market segment and creating your *Prospect Fishbowl*, you will want to gather names from observation, personal involvement within the market segment and from referrals and endorsements given to you by other people. Although your focus of "gathering names" will eventually change to "migrating" among the market, you will always want to maintain your effort to continually upgrade your *Prospect Fishbowl* with new names. If you don't, you will eventually find that your skill level exceeds your market access level and your enthusiasm, plus your income will be limited. Continually adding prospects to your *Prospect Fishbowl* is imperative. It allows you to eliminate prospects that don't fit your skill level without fear of depleting your selling opportunities by reducing the quantity of potential prospects. At the same time, it allows you to upgrade your *Prospect Fishbowl* with better prospects that utilize your skill level more frequently and builds your competency and confidence.

you will always want to maintain your effort to continually upgrade your Prospect Fishbowl with new names

One of the ways of upgrading your *Prospect Fishbowl* is through the acquisition of referrals and endorsements. Both sources require the participation of someone who regards you favorably. The higher the regard for who you are, or the higher your perception as the "Brand of Choice" *(Identity Brand)* within your market segment, the greater the likelihood that you will be successful in this endeavor.

Referrals are simply names of prospects attained from an individual who felt comfortable enough to provide them. Getting referrals of any significant

Getting referrals...requires a conscious and proactive effort. It happens because you make it happen.

magnitude always requires a conscious and proactive effort. It happens because you make it happen. Those who don't get referrals, have only themselves to fault. Referrals do not just come on their own, regardless of your length of time in business or your prestige in the community. They come because you ask.

When you get into a discussion about referrals, always identify your prospect profile to the referrer so that the names fit your skill level. If you aren't always protective of your ideal prospect profile you will violate it. If you aren't protective, even if, by accident, you will find yourself getting involved working with prospects that are below your skill level and you will limit your income potential.

One way of maintaining the integrity of your prospect profile is to carry a laminated card the size of a business card that lists the two most important characteristics of your profile, plus the number of referrals you are requesting. As your experience, age and specialization in your field change, you will find that your prospect profile will change as well. Usually, the most important criteria of any prospect profile are income, whether it is individual or family, net worth, if you are working the estate market, and market segment affiliation. The only exceptions are if you are working a product-specific specialty where the product requires certain buyer criteria such as an age requirement for long-term care insurance or business ownership for 401(k) retirement plans. Other criteria are dependent on the market segment that you are trying to penetrate, personal preference or the requirements that you need to maintain for the narrower focus of a proclaimed specialty.

One of the reasons that laminated cards listing your prospect profile work so well is that the majority of people in the world are "visually oriented." They would rather see a map than read written directions. They would rather see a demonstration, how something is done, rather than read or hear about how it should be done. The best managers of new people in any organization always couple "in-house" training with "field experience" that shows the new skill. New attorneys watch senior attorneys. New waitresses and waiters follow around experienced ones to see demonstrated what they have been taught, how to serve customers. Your best result in getting what you want is to "show them." Hand them the profile-card and let them feel it and see it while they think. Include the number of referrals that you want to obtain on the card. Implementing this one idea will bring to you a new level of success in obtaining referrals.

the majority of people in the world are "visually oriented."

You may also want to use a referral duplication form for recording referral names, promising to give them a copy when you leave. This provides an assurance for the referrer that you value his or her input and respect the importance of these names. You may suggest that he or she call these people before you do or promise that you will include them on a regular newsletter-mailing program for a period of time before contacting them. The duplication form is another reminder to emphasize to the referrer the prospect profile that you are seeking. Since the desired prospect characteristics are printed on the form, it is hard for either one of you to stray off the intended profile.

Examples of laminated cards and the referral duplication form are shown on the next two pages.

Laminated Referral Cards

**Business Owner / Professional
Income > $100,000
3 Names**

**Executive / Professional
Family Income > $90,000
4 Names**

Referral Duplication Form

Business Owner / Professional
Income_____

Name _____   Name _____

Phone _____   Phone _____

Info _____   Info _____

Name _____   Name _____

Phone _____   Phone _____

Info _____   Info _____

Name _____   Name _____

Phone _____   Phone _____

Info _____   Info _____

Name _____   Name _____

Phone _____   Phone _____

Info _____   Info _____

In choosing your market segment(s), if you have focused on and share the common denominators of the segment, which are cohesiveness, usually reflected by an occupational, lifestyle, social, or ethnic commonality, and the members maintain consistent communication between each other, you have a tremendous opportunity for attaining endorsements. Your personal commonality, in combination with the other denominators, gives you a significant advantage. If you have identified and influenced an "individualized" market segment by "giving" and not just "getting," the endorsement route is your most effective means for upgrading your *Prospect Fishbowl* as well as eventually gaining market access to desirable prospects.

Endorsements are the reverse of referrals and are usually the best method of maintaining the integrity of your prospect profile and in working within your skill level. It is simply the act of providing a name that you already have in your *Prospect Fishbowl*, which fits your prospect profile, and asking the referring person for

> *Endorsements are...the best method of...working within your skill level.*

information about the person and an endorsement to be used when you call on him or her. Your request should be similar to: *"Jack, here is a list of names (in the market segment that this person is familiar with) that I currently send newsletters to on a regular basis and invite to special events. Eventually, I will call on each one of them and I hope, over a period of time, a number of them will become clients. Could you take a minute and tell me whom I should call on first and, probably just as important, whom I should avoid. Your insights would be really valuable."*

Clearly state that you will eventually be calling on each one of them. You are not asking for a name. You are asking for information about the people you are going to call on. You even ask for those whom the referrer thinks would be a waste of time. That doesn't mean that you will remove them from your *Prospect Fishbowl.* You may find someone later who is this person's best friend and provides an incredible introduction, but it is amazing how many people will find it easy to start talking about who they don't like, and why, and then feel that they have to give you names of "good people" that you should call on just to redeem themselves. Let the referrer go in any direction he or she wants. You both will have fun. When the referrer is done, ask if you can mention his or her name when you call the prospect. Since you were the initiator of the name, permission is always granted.

What About the Effect of the Internet?

Bill Gates, Microsoft founder and one of the wealthiest men in the world today, said that you don't have to be able to predict the future, but you sure better pay attention to where it's headed. Wayne Gretsky, the greatest hockey player in history, was asked what had defined his remarkable playing career. He said that he learned early not to skate to where the puck

you need to start skating not to where the market is but to where the "marketplace will be"

was but to skate to where the puck was going to be. Well, you also need to start skating not to where the market is but to where the "marketplace will be" as Lynn B. Upshaw, author of *Building Brand Identity,* says. It will be the only game in town. It's a game of single elimination. If you lose this one, just go home. There are no prizes for second place.

Yes, the Internet will affect YOU and THIS business, not just everyone else. In the very near future the Internet will be accessible from everyone's cable TV box. Within five years, the Internet will be voice friendly and will allow your clients to converse with you face-to-face over the computer monitor or their TV screens. The technology is already available. Within two years, the monthly Internet access charge will drop to no more than the monthly cost of adding another movie channel to your cable TV; within five years or less, you will have full Internet access with interactive face-to-face capability with no monthly fee.

When this occurs, infomercials won't advertise a telephone number in order to be able to talk to the psychic hotline. You will be able to simply point the infrared TV changer to the "contact us" square on the screen and you will be connected with your personal psychic in a face-to-face chat, a personal relationship!

A lot of traditional appointments in which one drives to the other's office or home, will be eliminated. If I, the consumer, want to avoid further intrusion during my nonworking hours, I will ask that we meet over the Internet to discuss what you are proposing. To prosper, the sales professional of the future will learn to conduct many of his or her interviews by this means. You can look at this change as an opportunity or a problem. Different sales professionals will view it differently, but all who survive will have to adapt.

What are the problems and threats that this new technology will represent to you? First of all, it won't be just term insurance that gets sold over the Internet.

When companies can contact prospects with a face-to-face encounter over the Internet, through their

it won't be just term insurance that gets sold over the Internet

TV screen, they will definitely go after and capture a portion of market share. Companies will have rooms of cubicles filled with marketers in their national headquarters (e-commerce technology calls them "Customer Relationship Management Centers). Those marketers' job will be to make face-to-face contact with their customers for either service or "good will" and then attempt to cross sell other products. What we refer to today, as alternative distribution channels, will create a major impact. If shares in your financial company are publicly traded on the stock exchange, obtaining

obtaining business by e-commerce (Internet) will not be a choice!

business by e-commerce (Internet) will not be a choice! Sooner or later, a lack of e-commerce will hurt the company's credibility and their stock price. E-commerce must become a significant distribution channel for attaining increased profits and return on equity (ROE). The methods employed by these companies for attaining this business will become highly creative.

How many of your clients have a major credit card from a company that, in the future, will offer, "financial planning" advice? It will be an easy task for companies to access their own client base over the Internet. Think about American Express and how many of your clients have their card. Would you want to bet on whether a customer relationship manager contacts them about financial products through interactive technology over the Internet, on their TV screen, within the next five years? What about the banks whose customers are also yours and have now merged with insurance companies? Your clients, as well as prospects, will have numerous opportunities to personally interface with people competing for what you thought was your business. The contacts will be over the Internet, but through the average persons TV and they will be personal. The consumer will now have an alternative to what we once believed could never be replaced with anything but a living, walking, breathing salesperson.

Just last week my credit card company called to communicate that they had noticed unusual activity on my credit card and wanted to verify that it wasn't stolen. They noticed charges from out of the country and as a courtesy, were calling to verify that these were indeed my charges. After I verified that they were indeed mine, I was then led through a discussion about their credit card protection plan and asked to sign up. After that, I was asked about other credit card balances that I might want to transfer to them based on their new promotional rate. Do you really think that this all started due to a "courtesy call" to verify charges, or due to a planned and intentional cross-selling corporate strategy? Imagine that in the near future, during a "courtesy call," they will ask if they can send an email package on financial planning and products that may be of interest. A lot of people will say, "yes" to that offer. A follow-up phone call from a technology communication "specialist" (a customer relationship manager) a week later may provide some rather amazing results.

I am sure that companies will eventually send email information packages to all of their clients as the company databases become more refined. *Sales and Marketing* magazine, December 1999, in a special technology article entitled *"No Turning Back"*, author Ginger Conlon, says, "Forget rejoicing over a 2 percent direct mail response rate, and start expecting something a little higher, say 40 percent...that's the level of response many business-to-business email marketers are

> *I am sure that companies will eventually send email information packages to all...clients*

experiencing." When your database can indicate when a prospect is most apt to have available cash for purchases, such as a child finally getting out of college, a home mortgage being paid off or a large gain on a stock transaction, you can attain response levels higher than ever imagined. Database marketing will eventually affect your entire market and all consumers. It will even be used by charitable organizations to determine the best time to solicit someone about a sizeable contribution. They will be able to see the financial signals that indicate that "now" is the best predictive time to make the solicitation contact.

Calls from these customer relationship managers to your clients are not courtesy calls. They are creative strategy calls for directly cross selling their other products. And the email introduction packages are not just introduction packages; they are interactive programs that allow you to click on a reply icon to request more specific information, a comparison or a quote. You will see what used to be dubbed "computer phone bank" operations now set up as "Customer Relationship Management Centers" in major companies. Licensed operators, trained in how to sell and how to effectively handle the email and interactive responses, will staff them. Ask USAA Life if it works. It will work even better when you are able to make an initial contact that appears to be a "high concern" relationship contact about the prospect's personal credit card safety or some other creative issue. Your clients and prospects are going to be pursued by many new players. E-commerce will be a distribution channel in most, if not all, companies that will be accountable for producing significant results. The communication technology will not replace personal relationships; it will provide an appealing alternative, a "direct contact" personal relationship. The cover story on *Business Week*, June 28, 1999, said, "Any company that relies on a traditional sales force will have to do some soul searching...companies are finding that they need new skills..." I would suggest that the individual sales professional needs new skills as well.

So, what is the positive side of technology? Can there be advantages for the local salesperson derived through this new medium of communication? The answer is yes! In the magazine, *Strategy and Business,* Fourth Quarter 1999, an article entitled "The Internet as a Marketing Medium", Frank Ingari, comments that companies better begin recognizing that "...the web is likely to be the center of their marketing future, not simply an adjunct to traditional marketing methods." The issue is that you, the sales associate, as well as the companies, better start deciding "HOW", not if, you will use the Internet in your marketing efforts. Dan Sullivan, author of *The 21st Century Agent,* writes, "...those who operate as entrepreneurs and who use micro technology to their competitive advantage will succeed." He goes on to say, "The entire global economy is going

> *you...better start deciding "HOW", not if, you will use the Internet in your marketing efforts*

electronic faster than anyone can comprehend...the ability to navigate within this universe and to create value...is now the key to personal and professional success..."

Internet technologies will neither replace all sales professionals nor make them dispensable, but it will produce a major change in the way you will have to conduct business. The Internet may, in fact, be the sales professional's best way to stay current, communicate and sell more to their clients. The traditional argument that "face-to-face contact can never be replaced with anything that will get the same results and, therefore, I need not concern myself" is too simplistic in today's market place.

There will always be clients and prospects, termed "relationship delegators," who will want a local sales professional, but even these clients and prospects will have grown weary of the everyday constant intrusions on their time. The sales professional that can save them time by occasionally accessing them with a face-to-face encounter over the Internet, instead of always in person, will appear much more contemporary and have an advantage over the competition. Many will regard this ability as critical in their choice of establishing or even maintaining a business relationship. The very least a client or prospect will expect is your ability to send an *Email Concept™* information package on the new idea that you want to discuss with them as well as any other general information, announced events and newsletters through email. This is all available today! The prospect's condition of entry into the relationship will be your ability to communicate with them via the Internet/communication systems. This is not an issue that you can afford to ignore. Clients and prospects are no longer patient while you are catching up. They don't need to be. There are lots of new alternatives. Today's consumer wants what they want, when they want it and they expect you to provide it. You don't have to be able to predict the future but, as Peter Drucker says, "We must pay attention to survive."

If you can individualize your specific market segment, Identity Brand your reputation to capture "mindshare," and then add collaborative database marketing, you will create an emotional bond with your consumer that will be practically impossible to break. According to Wally Dale, author of *Collaborative Database Marketing*, only six percent of American households bought insurance directly in 1998; however, "In 5 years, though, predictions are that 38% will buy directly." Dale says, "As your organization moves to collaborative database marketing, it's important to keep using what has been working for you, but start immediately using the tools of technology to transition to the future."

...start accumulating email addresses of clients and prospects NOW!

To begin the process, start accumulating email addresses of clients and prospects NOW! You can begin assembling a database through a collaborative questionnaire sent once a year to your clients and prospects. Wally Dale, in *Collaborative Database Marketing*, has a great example for the insurance industry. A modified example of this questionnaire is included at the end of this chapter (see page 111). The person in charge of the database would record the information gathered as well as the prospect and client's email addresses. A marketing manager could initially be the person in charge of the database as well as coordinating the marketing efforts and communication within your office. Another alternative would be to send a database questionnaire

Technology is the transition to the future. If you...decide not to play, you will lose this game.

mailed through your home office in premium notices, magazines and annual reports. The hard data, as well as email addresses, could be collected and recorded, and then sent back to the marketing manager. As life events create "raise your hand" responses to the information provided to the clients, the responses could be sent back to the field office for follow-up. Regardless of which method is chosen, an email database in the future will be necessary to meet client expectations. Both methods will require that the field person be proficient in video teleconferencing with their contacts over the Internet. As this process develops, Wally Dale believes that eventually it will lead to an unbundling of the sales process with the sales professionals spending "the majority of their time in front of clients who have requested appointments." Technology is the transition to the future. If you don't pay attention or if you decide not to play, you will lose this game.

When the Internet allows companies to talk face-to-face with the client or prospect, you will see more future business go direct than you ever imagined, unless you have distinctively captured the "mindshare" of the person. Yes, it will happen. Some of these competing companies may be your own home offices. Some will justify the direct contact with your clients in the future as necessary to capture sales that would have gone undetected. They will justify the contact as necessary to reduce unit cost while increasing their return on equity (ROE) in order to maintain a profitable product portfolio. Your protection is to have uniquely captured your prospect's "mindshare" and to have created preference for YOU, a local *Identity Brand.*

Lynn Upshaw, in *Building Brand Identity,* says, "When the strategic personality and positioning have been successfully blended the *you must integrate technology to survive this next round of competition*

result is a brand essence that is hard for prospects to ignore." You must build your own "brand essence" and you must integrate technology to survive this next round of competition. Technology and Identity Branding your reputation to your individualized, local markets are not mutually exclusive, rather they are complementary. One without the other will not meet the needs of the future client. Together, they can capture market share and increase productivity. The following story may help you to visualize this new future.

A Story From The Future

It's a day in the year 2006. Jack just got home from work. The competition on the job is more and more intense. Every company seems to want more and more out of less and less to increase their profit margins in order to stay competitive. After dinner, Jack goes to the AOL Web TV. Although introduced in June of 2000, it didn't really catch on until two to three years later. It is amazing how it has evolved over the last three years. Jack uses it all the time for almost everything. Most people do. The Internet is now part of the basic service cost for cable TV so there is no longer a separate cost for accessing the Internet. It's been like that for five years now. And the interactive shopping channels make it so easy to buy almost anything that you need. They only require pointing the remote control and a quick "click." Jack has agreed to be interviewed on how the Internet changed his and his family's life. Here are a few excerpts from that interview.

Q: Tell me how Internet communication has affected your family.

A: Well, we use it for everything now, shopping, vacations, groceries, talking to our friends, etc. It is also the first thing that any of us check whenever we have been away from the house or when I get home every evening, kind of like how you used to check your telephone answering machines. Wow, that's showing my age, isn't it? Now that your phone messages connect through the Internet, it's so much easier to see who called before you even retrieve the message. You can prioritize how you pick them up or which ones you just discard. Even my Mom and Dad use it with all of their friends, now. It is so easy to use, especially since it is connected through the TV cable.

Q: What are some other examples of how Internet access via TV has influenced your family.

A: I can sure tell you that Mom, who is 76 years old, has caught on. I guess with learning to use the ATM machines at the bank she finally figured out that her favorite show, QVC shopping network, wasn't any more complicated. She says that it became even more fun to watch once she could "click" and buy. I think she is addicted. She still marvels at how they merged the TV, phone and computer all into one. She used to be afraid of the "computer in the box." Now, it's just part of her TV and easy to use!

Q: What about your dad? Does he use Internet TV also?

A: Oh, man, my Dad thinks it's great that he can talk to the travel agent over the TV set now and plan his and Mom's next trip. He planned a trip with Mom to London last year and by the time he was done communicating with the travel agent on TV, I think he made a new best friend. He even talks to his stockbroker like that now. They talk and view stock charts together over the TV (check out: Webex.com. The service is free NOW). He never really liked trading on-line but he loves talking to his broker even though each trade is $29.95. He is a little embarrassed when he sees his former broker at church, but that guy just never adapted to the new technology. To make the trips over to his former broker's office just got to be too inconvenient. And Dad hates people coming to his home to sell stuff to him. Actually, I think that everyone does. Anyway, Dad loves this new Web TV technology. I'm not even sure that his former broker is in the business anymore. You know, I don't think he was old enough to have retired. Oh, well...I guess things just happen.

Q: Were you surprised that your parents adapted so quickly to AOL Web TV?

A: Who would have ever guessed that the older generation would take to this like they did. I guess we never thought about the mobility issues that this technology resolved or how easy it would become to use. Dad even does the grocery shopping now. He loves the virtual shopping aisles that he wheels his virtual shopping cart down and then the pointing and clicking. Plus, they credit his bill with all the national coupons (check out: Lowesfoodtogo.com or Grocer.net – It is all available NOW!). I think he feels like he is in control. Oh, yeah, he always talks to the Internet grocer, even if to just say hi. You'd think that they were also best friends. Who ever thought that relationships would be easier to develop on the Internet than in person? Well, I guess they are communicating in person aren't they?

Q: *Have they bought a lot of other products or services over the AOL Web TV?*

A: *He told me that the other day his insurance company, that is now part of The Big National Bank, contacted him through email over his TV. I think they issue his credit card, too. Anyway, I don't really know who called him, the bank, the insurance company or the credit card people. Nevertheless, it was a face-to-face, good-will service contact by TV email. Pretty cool! They sent him an interactive email presentation through the TV on some information that he could click through. He liked it and clicked on the request block to talk to a representative to answer some questions. The representative was on Web TV within seconds! Dad really liked the guy, said he was as personable as his agent, plus it was just so convenient to talk personally over the TV. He didn't even have to leave a voice mail for the guy to get back to him. Don't you hate having to leave voice mails and hope someone will call you back? This was instantaneous. That is hard to beat.*

> **Who ever thought that relationships would be easier to develop on the Internet than in person?**

Q: *Is his insurance agent still around?*

A: *Oh, his agent is still around, but he doesn't think that his agent will ever find out that he purchased an annuity from this TV guy. Plus, it's just a business deal. It's not that he doesn't like him anymore; he does. But it's not like his agent is an old college roommate or they see each other a lot. He also told this Web TV representative to contact me with information on a college education fund for the new twins. Dad is always trying to help. I guess that never ends.*

Q: Did the guy call you?

he asked if he could send me an interactive email package over the Internet

A: Yes. He did call. He seems like a really nice guy. I told him that I worked with a financial planner and he said that was usually the norm, but then he asked if he could send me an interactive email package over the Internet that I could click through that might provide some helpful information on college planning.

Q: And did he send it?

A: Oh yeah... and it was great! I didn't have to go to a Web site. It just came through on my email screen. It allowed me to click through five or six pages. I was impressed with all the information I could access so easily. (Note: These are available now, called Email Concepts™) He called me back about a week later and we talked over the AOL Web TV so that we could see each other plus the information at the same time. He said that most of their clients really like reviewing stuff like this in this way and that they had been doing it for about four years now. You know, they have got to be a great company to be this advanced.

Q: What about your financial planner?

A: My planner is a really good guy, but this was really neat stuff. You know, I just don't have the time to make an appointment, as my planner always wants me to. I wonder why my guy doesn't contact me like this. I guess that most local agents all work pretty much the same. Not very hi-tech, huh? Makes you wonder if maybe the company isn't very up-to-date either. You know, years ago he told me that I would always want a personal agent but between these interactive email packages and AOL Web TV,

between...interactive email packages and AOL Web TV, you can't get much more personal.

you can't get much more personal. You know, he should really start doing this or he could lose a lot of business, don't you think?

Q: **Why did you say that the company might not be up-to-date and not just the agent?**

A: *Well, I think they're a good company. They are one of the top ten in size, anyway. But I still get print mail from them on everything. No one, not my agent or the company has ever sent an email reply to my few questions, much less informed me through interactive email packages about products, updates, or anything. Sure, they have a Web site, but don't they have their client's email addresses. I mean, everyone's email address has been in the email phone directory at switchboard.com for four years now and...(pause)...nothing! (Note: Check out switchboard.com. It, or something similar, will replace your hardcopy phone book within the next five years.) Forget about them even thinking about this Web TV thing! How can a company be this far behind? Makes you wonder about their products and everything. If I were the planner, I'd find a different company...or maybe I should find a different planner.*

Q: **Well, I can't help you there. Tell me what else your dad liked about the Web TV bank rep he spoke with on AOL TV?**

A: *Oh, yeah, they invited my dad to an investment presentation with some big investment company. They say that they do that every quarter. He will love that! Who knows, I may*

> **they...have a live Web TV conference each week for their local clients to tune into**

go with him. He invited me. Oh, and they also have a live Web TV conference each week for their local clients to tune into. Kind of neat when you have an investment hour each week on the stuff that you own.

Q: *What do you think that your financial planner would say if he knew that you were going with your dad to the investment presentation?*

A: *I think he would probably be upset. But Dad's right, he probably wouldn't even know. I wonder how he's doing now with the banks, CPAs and everyone doing the same thing. Plus, now with AOL Web TV, gosh, Dad really likes that convenience. I do, too. Anyway, I hope that he is doing OK, but this new relationship building on Web TV is just too* **but this new relationship building on Web TV is just too convenient for people not to get involved with...** *convenient for people not to get involved with it. Anyway, it's got to be hard for him.*

Q: *Why else do you sense that your agent might be having a hard time?*

A: *Well, selling an intangible product is pretty hard. I mean the products are all virtually the same with all companies. At least I can't see any difference. It's not like a car where you can see something that is visibly distinct, you know, something that you just have to have.*

Q: *But selling financial products was always an intangible sale. Why do you think that its harder today?*

A: *Well, now that the banks and everyone else are contacting everyone directly, it's really got to be tough. Plus, now they offer these big investment events plus the Web TV weekly reviews to keep you up to date. Did I tell you that a specialty "cruise only" travel company is cosponsoring this next investment event with a special presentation about the Greek Islands? That kind of grabs your attention and I could even get my wife to go to something like that even with the investment stuff – which she hates! It makes it more like an entertainment evening and not a seminar.*

Q: Does your financial planner offer things like this to go to?

A: You probably can't do that as an individual agent, at least I don't know of anyone who does things like that locally. And no one would do it consistently, at least no one that I, or any of my friends, know of. It's got to be hard to get people to notice you. It's got to be tough, don't you think?

*Q: **Why do you think that he doesn't spend more time trying to do at least some things like this? I would think that his company would help him.***

A: Well, speaking in his defense, I think he probably spends most of his time looking for a new customer. I mean it's tough out there. He's probably trying to survive. Maybe that's why he has always asked me for a new name whenever I do see him. But it's tough to give a name when you have "direct contact" personal relationships offered like this over AOL Web TV now. I know that I would think twice about having a personal agent when I could get the convenience of the

I don't know why my planner didn't get involved with this new technology.

...he shouldn't have waited.

"instant Rep" on Web TV. This business has to be tough. I don't know why my planner didn't get involved with this new technology. Why didn't he do that? Do you think he just didn't see it coming? His company should have helped him, don't you think? But he shouldn't have waited. He just should have gotten involved somehow. What do you think? It's got to be tough.

The END

To remain competitive in the future, it will be necessary to take an intangible product and recreate it into a "package of value," whose main characteristic is its consistent visibility to the client and prospect. Some refer to this as a tangible service product. The only way to accomplish this is by developing prospect familiarity through creative and repetitive events, unique contacts and unique services. Technology will be important to this future strategy. Without the ability to access your clients and prospects

> *it will be necessary to take an intangible product and recreate it into a "package of value," whose main characteristic is its consistent visibility to the client and prospect. Some refer to this as a tangible service product.*

through the available communication technology, you won't be able to maintain your competitive advantage. The ability to interface with the customer on a personal basis through the Internet communication systems will be imperative.

Creating a Web site will not be the solution for making you appear unique and distinct. It will not create an Identity Brand that differentiates you from the competition. Web sites may provide visual proof that you are technologically proficient; they may become necessary for providing client service, allowing clients a method to make instant changes to a flexible product that they own; they may even provide a point-of-sale advantage, but a Web site will not create prospect attraction for the person who has never met you.

Only those representatives and offices that adopt Internet communication technology as a partner in their marketing strategies, will survive. You will need the ability and skills to display presale material to the client during a phone conversation on his or her computer screen or be able to forward it to their email as an *Email Concept* with an agreement to call back later to discuss the information. A shared computer screen, between two or more parties while conversing over the phone line, is a free service that anyone can access now. It can even be interactive. Check out: www.Webex.com. In the near future, you will need the ability to visually interact over the computer screen or the Web TV screen, while displaying written information on a split screen. All of these technologies are presently available and used internally in many companies. They will be widespread within five years. In the near future, technology will integrate the TV, telephone and computer all into one package. It is going to happen fast.

The salespeople who survive in the future will not, in five to ten years, even be identifiable to their predecessors of today. The personal sales representative will not be extinct, but success will require building direct relationships through entirely new communication systems. In many cases, your personal contact with a client or even a prospect will be through the interactive Internet or not at all. People, who want high-touch, personal relationships with their professionals will demand and expect alternatives to meeting with you. Time issues, business demands, privacy and convenience will require your ability to build personal relationships over the Internet. If you can't accommodate the way he or she wants to communicate, your client will leave for someone who can.

your personal contact with a client or even a prospect will be through the interactive Internet or not at all

If you don't believe that technology will take a large piece of the market, remember that neither did anyone believe that selling sophisticated computers directly over the phone without a face-to-face salesperson could create a large company. Well just ask Dell® Computer, who generates millions in revenues on a daily basis how their strategy worked out. Now, what were your thoughts about financial service companies not being able to make much of an impact by going direct or clients not being receptive?

If you believe that you can survive by essentially doing what you are doing now, you need to ask yourself what assumptions you are making that will need to hold true for that to happen. Then ask yourself, what would need to happen to make your assumptions invalid.

The bottom line is that you can't ignore technology if you are going to survive. You can't fight it and neither can you resist adapting. You must find the technology link to relationship marketing in the future or your

Technology and marketing may once have been viewed as strange bedfellows, no longer!

business will languish, if not fail. Technology and marketing may once have been viewed as strange bedfellows, no longer!How will you begin to accumulate an email database? What else will you do to stay abreast of the communication /technology opportunities?

How will you begin to accumulate an email database? What else will you do to stay abreast of the communication/technology opportunities?

Robert E. Krumroy

Please take a few minutes to give us your thoughts about financial services and information that may be of continual interest to you. We will record this in our communication system so we can give you appropriate information and invite you to appropriate events. We would also like to know what your preference is on the way we can communicate with you. Our promise is that we will respond only with the information you want in the way you want it. (Fold and return)

Name:_____Date: _____
Home Phone: _____Business: _____Fax: _____
E-mail Address: _____
Address:_____City/State/Zip: _____
Occupation: _____Date of Birth: _____
Spouse: _____
Occupation: _____Date of Birth: _____
Business Phone: _____Fax: _____

Children:
Name: _____DOB: _____Name: _____DOB: _____
Name: _____DOB: _____Name: _____DOB: _____

What communication method would you prefer we use to get important information to you?
E-mail: _____yes / Fax: _____ yes / Reg. mail to home: _____ yes / Mail to work: _____ yes

Please answer the following questions:
Would you like to receive our 1-page monthly financial newsletter?   Yes _____ No_____
Would you like to be invited to attend (free) periodic investment
events by national economists, fund managers and other specialists
that we sponsor locally?   Yes_____ No_____

In the last or next 12 months, changes in my life are as follows:
New family members   Yes_____ No_____
Children starting college or graduating   Yes_____ No_____
Divorce   Yes_____ No_____
Disability   Yes_____ No_____
Death   Yes_____ No_____
Job change   Yes_____ No_____
Retirement   Yes_____ No_____
Change in debt   Yes_____ No_____
Inheritance   Yes_____ No_____
Job changed - 401(K) distribution   Yes_____ No_____

Would you like information now or periodically on:
Investments?   Yes____ No____ Send info_____
Retirement planning?   Yes____ No____ Send info_____
College funding?   Yes____ No____ Send info_____
Information for company retirement money that is becoming available? Yes____ No____ Send info_____
Information on tax savings?   Yes____ No____ Send info_____

If you cannot work, because of injury, illness, retirement or death, is it important to have:
Income for yourself and family?   Yes____ No____ Send info_____
Your loans and mortgage paid?   Yes____ No____ Send info_____

Business (For Business Owners Only)
Is it important to review an "excess contribution" retirement plan
supplement so that the owners can contribute **additional money** to
his/her own retirement account?   Yes____ No____ Send info_____
Need information on business buy/sell agreements?   Yes____ No____ Send info_____
Need information on "selective executive" incentive
arrangements for selective key employees?   Yes____ No____ Send info_____

Is Specializing Your Road to Success?

Eventually, as sales representatives become more capable at what they do, they struggle with the issue of whether to specialize. Dr. Thomas Stanley, author of *Networking with the Affluent,* says, "If I go back and look at the hundreds and hundreds of case studies that we have, what I find is that most of the extraordinary sales professionals in America who target the affluent are specialists." Most sales professionals who have continued to climb to new heights of success eventually came to a crossroad where they knew that they needed to narrow their focus. Once they took that step (if it were done correctly), they have come to realize that the change did not cause a loss; it caused a gain. As they narrowed their market, they broadened their appeal. Specializing enabled them to focus their marketing efforts to a more specific group of prospects. Not only did the prospect gain, but the sales professional gained a higher level of personal satisfaction. They gained new enthusiasm for what they did; their life's work took on new meaning. So, why don't more sales professionals take the plunge? What holds them back from doing what they know would be best for their careers?

> *As they narrowed their market, they broadened their appeal.*

In the beginning stage of business, most new sales entrants sell to anyone whom they can get to listen. As their business and skills develop, they become more selective. Many feel that eventually as much as

> *if not dealt with, you will eventually become the senior agent who feels like a "de-fanged lion."*

eighty percent of their customer base become clients whose future needs require a talent or skill that is well below their progressed talent level. It causes an emotional struggle. Do I provide the service and consistent contact that I originally promised or do I eventually lose contact, which means my initial clients become abandoned or underserved? The answer is not as simple as some would lead you to believe. It is an emotional issue but, if not dealt with, you will eventually become the senior agent who feels like a "de-fanged lion." Your new sales eventually will suffer and you will become emotionally and psychologically trapped. You start to lose faith in your own ability and wonder with self-doubt if you can elevate your customer base. It becomes a lingering atrophy. You know that you are capable of so much more, but there are no more hours in the day. You have no more time! There seems to be no way out. Your integrity won't allow you to abandon the clients that created your initial success. You have become a highly paid service clerk. You know that you have lost the vision and fulfillment in what you do. The price of continuing to ignore the direction of your current journey is too high, especially when there are strategies that can solve all of these issues.

Specialist vs. Generalist

Making the decision to become a specialist, is an acknowledgement that one can't or isn't willing to continue being all things to all people. It is a statement that he or she has decided to do what they do best and to do it more often. For most of these sales

Becoming a "specialist"... resolved an agonizing struggle.

Now they...wonder, "Why didn't I do it sooner?"

professionals, it was no small decision. It resolved an agonizing struggle. Having to decide what to "give up" and then imagining the potential impact or loss in income that could occur, even if only temporarily, was an emotional issue. Now they look back and wonder, "Why didn't I do it sooner?"

The market segments that value specialization the most are twofold: 1) those who perceive their needs to be distinctly different from the masses and believe that they are really understood by only a few and

2) those who represent the wealthiest segment of society, who insist on specialized service providers and, usually, have no tolerance for nonperformance. Both of these groups will be more attracted to a specialist and will pay more for the assurance that they are working with a specialist than worry about price or quibble over whose product is "best." To them, the security in "knowing," though based on perception, that their provider is a specialist implies a distinct advantage and higher confidence level than the generalist can provide. Consequently, if the generalist becomes involved in competition with this segment, he or she will, more times than not, lose to the perceived specialist. Even the generalist who knows that he has a higher knowledge level and can help the client with a better solution will be at a disadvantage. He will normally lose.

The alternative to specializing is aiming for everyone. When you are aiming for everyone, no one seems to come into focus very well. As the saying goes, "When you try to appeal to everyone, you appeal to no one." Gerald R. Baron, author of *Friendship Marketing*, says, "Marketers instinctively understand you can't be all things to all people, but the traditional salesperson wants to argue with, 'Why not, if I can get the commission?' On the other hand, highly productive salespeople have a knack of determining very quickly how well both their skill level and their offerings match the customer's needs. If the match isn't there, they move on until they find that match."

> *When you are aiming for everyone, no one seems to come into focus very well.*

Creating a Customer Service Enhancement

The first issue in deciding to specialize is deciding how to service the clients that no longer fit your market profile. There are numerous solutions to this issue. The first point is to realize that you are probably under servicing these people now. Even though you have a lot of files, don't let it create an illusion of security. You may be handling service requests, but proactive contact as well as profitability may be practically nonexistent. If these people could be handed over to a designated "customer service representative" who could be introduced as an enhancement to your practice, the clients would perceive that you are growing and increasing service, even service to them! If the customer service representative could be introduced as **their** customer service representative, who then sent out periodic newsletters, birthday cards, yearly database questionnaires and handled personally requested changes, the client would actually increase their loyalty to you. Even if the customer service representative were located elsewhere, much like the banks have regional service centers today, the clients would not know nor care. The majority of service work could be taken off of your shoulders.

The job of the customer service representative would be to insulate you from contact. Even future product interest on the part of the client or a review request would be qualified before giving it over to you for your consideration. At that time, you could decide to get involved or to pass it on to a junior associate for a commission split. If the customer service representative were local and licensed, you could even negotiate a commission split on the case with him or her, assuming that he or she can

The job of the customer service representative... insulate you from contact.

handle it without your involvement. If your office doesn't have a customer service representative, I would suggest creating one with other associates. Assign your block of business to the FULL-TIME customer service representative (not a part-time agent and part-time service rep – it doesn't work) and pay him a fifty-fifty split of your two percent service fees and twenty percent on additional sales that he uncovers on this block of business. You would be surprised how many sales a customer service representative can come up with when the incentive is motivating. It alleviates your service problems to a market that you have outgrown but keeps you in the loop for that "once-in-a-while surprise" when fortune prevails and one of your old clients does have a BIG opportunity for you to get involved in, if you only knew about it. Everyone wins and now you can focus your efforts on the top twenty percent of your client base. You've created a customer service enhancement for your existing client base, while being well on your way to establishing your new identity as a specialist.

The Benefit Is More Than Financial

Once you have dealt with the service issue for your existing client base, how can you be assured that "specializing" is your wisest decision? Narrowing your market and becoming a segment specialist always creates the highest level of customer appeal and corresponding income. It is no different than an orthopedic surgeon who attracts more people with sports injuries than a general doctor does. Who makes more money, the generalist who

becoming a segment specialist...creates the highest level of customer appeal

broadens his market more or the specialist who narrows his market further? Think about the brain surgeon! The narrower your market, the greater your appeal. Don't fool yourself. The road to success is not in increasing your product breadth. It is not in learning how to pick up all the loose change on the table. It is in your decision to narrow your focus and broaden your appeal.

When shopping malls were first created, they were built around large department stores that were referred to as anchor tenants. Today's shopping malls are built around specialty stores. Which has more appeal, The Gap or Dillards? Victoria's Secret or J.C. Penney? If you could buy stock in Sears or Home Depot, which would you choose? It is said that if you want to gaze into the crystal ball to see how any industry is going to move into the future, just look at retail. Retail is said to always incur the first casualties when the buying patterns of the public begin to change. The consumer is demanding more specialties, not fewer. Unless you want to be a discounter, specializing is how retail will survive and how the most successful professionals will position themselves for the future.

It's Who You Are...Not What You Sell!

Theodore Levitt, in his book *The Marketing Imagination,* says that to successfully sell in the future will require "more and more intensified relationships". The consumer will be attracted by a view of distinction, not product. Your appeal will no longer rest on product needs. Appeal will be based on perception of "who you are," not "what you sell." The perception of "who you are" or your attractiveness to the prospect is not something that your company can do for you, nor does it have anything to do with the level of your company's national name recognition. "Brand is more than a name. It represents a relationship customers have come to know and value," says Regis McKenna, author of *Real Time.* A company's name recognition may help with credibility once a purchase decision is being made by the prospect but it is *brand personality* that attracts the client and *brand personality* is created in the local market. Theodore Levitt goes on to say that "Success goes to those who differentiate themselves [not their product] in ways that attract...superior numbers of customers to themselves." For the consumer, making a decision to grant an interview or to purchase a product is going to be far more dependent on impression than on fact and that impression is going to be locally dependent.

brand personality...attracts the client and...is created in the local market

It will be you who will be responsible for creating a local market presence with a distinction, a *brand essence* that creates prospect

117

appeal; a reputation that is visibly different and unique relative to the competition. After all, "specialists" who are truly specialists are capable of being identified by their "not yet clients," their prospects, not just their present clients. If your prospects can't identify your specialty, you don't have one. If your prospects can't identify your specialty, your specialty will perform poorly in meeting your income and business goals.

How Do I Choose a Specialty?

So, how do you create a distinction around you and your chosen specialty? First, decide what your personal strengths and interests are in the business. Chances are that they will be the same. Secondly, decide if your personal interest is measured more in the product category or a demographic category. A specialty does not have to be based on a core product or an advanced service. Not everyone has to become a small business specialist working with nonqualified plans. Neither do you have to base a specialty on a product focus such as disability income, investments or 401(k) retirement plans. A specialty can be just as effective by being based on a deep and genuine concern to serve a certain category of client. Imagine the identity that could be built if you operated under the name "Korean Only Financial" and limited your work to the Korean population of your city. Do you think that segment could be attracted to your focus? Would you have an easier task of focusing in on how to develop your reputation with this identified and "individualized" group? Lynn Upshaw says, in *Building Brand Identity*, "Smart brand marketers rethink who their targets are by acknowledging that they are not targets at all, but individual human beings." In other words, you may be able to create some brand positioning with a name, but you can't build *brand personality* with a general group. The group must be individualized in order to create consumer attraction, which is the result of creating a *brand personality*.

There is a firm in California run by Richard Metcalfe that operates under the name "Seniors Only Financial." It is well known, not only by their clients but by their prospects, that they only work with clients over the age of fifty-five. Are they more expert than everyone else in this prospect market? Just ask the client. Better yet, get into competition with them over a prospect. You will more than likely lose before the competition even starts. Positioning has already been established. The name itself implies a higher level of expertise and specialty. The perception is well on its way to capturing the prospect's "mindshare." The *brand personality* is easy to target and Rick Metcalfe has done an incredible job. He knows who his prospects are and maintains a constant familiarization with them through all kinds of events and meaningful contacts. Some of his prospects have been influenced for months and even years before becoming clients. However, if you had asked them, even before they did business with Rick, who their specialist was, they would have answered..."Rick Metcalfe."

Harry Beckwith, author of *Selling the Invisible,* says, "Prospects do not buy how good you are at *what you do.* They buy how good you are at *who you are.*" Metcalfe is truly one of the gurus of creating a "quality perception" in the prospect's mind, and he follows through with quality service. He knows that it's not just name, not the company's and not his. Nor is what is promised or implied just smoke and mirrors. It takes substance, constant familiarization in unique ways, plus dedication to focus this narrowly and to become good at *"who you are."* Once it is accomplished successfully, everyone feels good. The final result benefits everyone. Rick owns this market today and probably in the future. He has no anxiety about where his sales will come from in the

> Harry Beckwith, author of Selling the Invisible, says, "Prospects do not buy how good you are at what you do. They buy how good you are at who you are."

future. He is **Identity Branded** as the specialist of choice not only to his clients but where it counts the most, to his prospects.

Creating an Automatic Advantage Over the Competition

What else can you do in order to increase your credibility as a specialist to your market segment? Most specialists would serve themselves well to create a *"distinction identifier"* that could help describe their positions to their market segments. This does not mean that you need a new business name or that you need to separate yourself from a large firm. Many, if not most, attorneys work under a firm name and still have distinct and recognizable specialties. A *distinction identifier* can

A distinction identifier...usually implies an advantage

be promoted to your market when conducting events, seminars and mailings. If possible, put it on your business card. In *Selling The Invisible,* Harry Beckwith, says, "If no prospect [notice that he does not say 'client'] can describe your position, you do not have one." A *distinction identifier* describes what you want your prospects to think. It is the initial qualifier that distinguishes you from your competitors. It usually implies an advantage. It is the initial impression that can go a long ways toward creating a perception of higher service, expertise and thus specialty...yours!

Identifying the core message of your distinctiveness with a brief sentence or phrase can become a central theme of your uniqueness to your market segment. Identifiers can describe for whom a unique service is offered. It can be simple or clever, but it definitely needs to identify you from "the pack." It needs to have a unique appeal to your market. Examples of *distinction identifiers* are:

- "Business Owners Only. An Exclusive Focus. A Greater Expertise."

- "Integrated Financial Strategies. A Longer Process. A Greater Benefit."

- "The Million Dollar Estate Specialist. When Reducing Taxes Matters."

- "The $100,000 Investment Specialist. A Larger Commitment. A Bigger Outcome."

- "Korean Only Financial. When an Exclusive Focus Makes a Difference."

Harry Beckwith, in *Selling The Invisible,* says, distinction statements that are true to what you do "will make your word of mouth more effective. They can rally your troops. They will get your marketing communications working as one." Decide on what your specialty focus is going to be and then make a distinctive statement. Don't make it too general. Statements such as "Plan Now. Secure Your Future" are not distinctive, serve no purpose and add no attraction power for your market segment. It doesn't imply any advantage over the competition and says nothing about your "specialty." Be specific, not general. If it is done right, you will gain a competitive edge. Just make sure that you can now support your statement. Make sure that you can deliver what you are going to promise.

Don't Ruin Your Perceived Image

...don't damage the market's perception of you as a specialist by once again looking like you "do it all."

Once you have decided to proclaim a specialty, don't ruin your perceived image by violating your new position. If you have proclaimed that you specialize ONLY in nonqualified plans, when asked if you handle group health insurance, the answer is

NO. It is fine to answer that you have an associate who is a specialist at group health and ask permission for he or she to call them. Negotiate a split with the other specialist, but by all means, don't damage the market's perception of you as a specialist by once again looking like you "do it all." Don't even ask for the census information.

The client's belief in your specialty will be greatly enhanced if you begin your dialogue by telling them what you don't do, what you are not a specialist in, what you have no clue about, before explaining what it is that you do specialize in. To illustrate this point, try telling someone, with no hint of humility, that your baseball-playing son is the number-one home run hitter in the state. They won't believe you! Now

You have to decide what it is that you no longer do and proclaim it as loudly as proclaiming your specialty.

try telling someone that your son plays baseball and is the worst on his team at judging and catching fly balls; that he is fully capable of missing the simplest catches. However, he is the number-one home run hitter in the state. They will now believe you! People always believe what it is you have to say after you tell them what it is that you are not good at. That is one of the critical issues in becoming a specialist. You have to decide what it is that you no longer do and proclaim it as loudly as proclaiming your specialty. Become a "finder" for services no longer in your specialty and delegate those services accordingly. Don't lose your focus. Your clients will be unforgiving.

In conclusion, there are four elements in properly moving into a specialty focus. First, determine your area of expertise. Be realistic, but make a leap into the future. Second, determine how to delegate your service work and determine a way to totally insulate yourself from contacts that are below your skill level. A customer service representative could be a major help. Third, determine a market segment to which your specialty appeals and then "individualize" your market. You can't make an impression or capture "mindshare" from a general audience or from an entire community, but if you identify by name those whom you would like to have as prospects, you can now focus your marketing communication effectively. You can create a *brand personality*. Remember that if your prospects (not clients) cannot describe your specialty, you don't have one. **Fourth**, create a visibility plan. How will you clearly communicate your specialty? How will you continually familiarize yourself to your market? What will you do to surprise the prospect and to look unique when compared to your competition? The future belongs not to those who have all the answers but to those who have a distinction. How will you, over time, successfully provide an answer to the prospect's question of "Why you?" before they have even had a face-to-face interview with YOU...the specialist.

The more alike an industry becomes, the more important a local distinction becomes. If you are distinct enough and continually visible to your market segment, even your nonclients (your prospects) will regard you as the mark of excellence in your field. Your job is to raise awareness and create a distinction, a *brand personality.*

Identity Branding is and will become as important a prerequisite to gaining prospect access in the future as a poker chip is necessary for entering a poker game. It doesn't guarantee success, but without it you will not even have a chance to play. Declaring a specialty can help create favoritism. It can give you a competitive edge. It can also rekindle your spark and enthusiasm for your career.

Write out what ideas you can adapt to narrow your focus and broaden your appeal to your market segment.

Little Items Can Build Brand Loyalty...or NOT

A critical issue for surviving the future is whether you can provide positive experiences to the prospects or clients in the way that they want them provided. The ways that they want them to be provided are changing quickly. There are two criteria here to consider. One of the criteria is "positive" and the other is "in the way that they want it." The evaluation of those conditions comes from the client or prospect, not from you.

If the client or prospect is not happy with how they are getting what they want, no explanation is going to build, sustain or enhance your Identity Brand. The perception of who you are and your differentiation to the competition is going to be

Once a good perception is created, the consumer's mind closes to new input that would allow for reconsideration, a major factor in brand loyalty.

irrevocably harmed. No one is going to care about your explanations about why they can't get what they want in the way that they want it. Once a negative perception is created, it is virtually impossible to change. However, the good news is that the opposite is also true. Once a good perception is created, the consumer's mind closes to new input that would allow for reconsideration, a major factor in brand loyalty.

If you regularly drink COKE® you don't care that you chose Pepsi® in the taste test at the supermarket. When they inform

Preference is always based on perception over fact.

you of your taste choice and hand you the half-price Pepsi coupon, sometime during your shopping excursion you will ignore the results, negate the explanations, not care about the price advantage and slide another twelve pack of COKE into your shopping basket. The facts don't matter. "Don't bother me with the facts! My mind is made up. I like COKE!" The lesson is to make sure that your prospects form positive perceptions of you very quickly. Preference is always based on perception over fact.

Lynn Upshaw, author of *Building Brand Identity,* says, "Brands have no right to exist". Brands are usually not created nor justified due to superior product. However, brands dominate product choice in our society. Brands account for over ninety percent of all products purchased in America. Brand dominance begins when the consumer is provided with experiences, which create impressions and result in capturing "mindshare." Brands stay dominant by maintaining consistent familiarity with positive experiences. People rely on only partial facts and initial impressions to make their initial judgments. Once judgments are made and brand preference is established, people rarely change their minds. Inadequate time, patience and lack of expertise usually discourage reconsideration, even when new facts are presented. It takes effort and emotion to make a decision. Even if imperfect, a decision helps to simplify the person's life. To reconsider other facts, which would challenge their initial decision, would require that they "recomplicate" their lives with more effort and more emotional stress. Why? They were comfortable with their initial decision.

Have you ever heard someone say, "Don't confuse me with the facts. My mind is made up." Brands provide the easiest way for consumers to simplify their lives in an information overloaded society. As long as consistent familiarization continues, in a way that pleases them, the consumer has no reason to change. Loyalty is established! Hopefully, their loyalty is connected to your Identity Brand.

Maintaining loyalty requires consistent familiarization. It also requires constantly asking yourself if there is any thing that you are doing, or not doing, that the consumer wishes you would change. For instance, how many of your clients or prospects would prefer having you communicate with them via the Internet versus receiving another printed mailing? Do you know the answer? A database questionnaire sent periodically to your clients would provide that type of information. With the daily barrage of junk-mail, this is no small matter for many consumers. How many people in your market segment wish that you would stop sending a printed newsletter and, instead, send them the newsletter by email? If you can't do that now, you either have the wrong newsletter or the wrong technology, because both are currently available. If you aren't moving from print to technology, some of your clients and prospects will be less than appreciative in the near future.

Not knowing what the client wants or not providing what the client wants in the way that he or she want it is far more critical today than at any other time in history. Clients expect what they want in the way they want it and they expect you to be responsive and current in meeting their expectations. Research and experience shows that at least forty percent of your prospects would prefer having newsletters sent by email instead of through the regular mail. Are you listening and responding? You need to know what your clients want. It will eventually make an impact to building or sustaining brand loyalty...positively or negatively.

Email Concepts...Are You Current?

How many times have you had a prospect say "no" to your request for an appointment? You really want to see this prospect or client but you have run into the proverbial brick wall. Sure, there are times when you should back off and call again in twelve months. If you include them as part of your structured branding plan, focusing on consistent familiarization, you can expect good future results. This familiarization can be achieved through newsletters (consider an email version), invitations to consistent unique events and even casual personal contacts that will naturally occur through your market segment interaction. However, before giving up on your phone request for an initial meeting, why not ask permission to forward an

Email Concept™, providing information about the problem or subject that you wanted to discuss.

Email Concept packages provide the prospect with basic, but brief, educational information on the unwanted financial consequences of not having a buy-sell, a supplemental deferred compensation plan for the owner, a 401(k) plan for the employees, an estate plan to eliminate devastating financial losses, a strategically customized financial plan that can maximize wealth and reduce unnecessary taxes and numerous other concepts within the financial services field. *Email Concepts* are problem focused, not solution focused. They provide the prospect value by providing an educational glimpse of the problem, not an intellectual description of the solution.

Email Concepts...provide the prospect value by providing an educational glimpse of the problem, not an intellectual description of the solution.

Prospects are hesitant about granting appointments when they lack information about the problem or they have no evidence of the sales professionals trustworthiness or competency. If the prospect or client will give you permission, send an *Email Concept* package about the idea. Instead of having to accept a "no" to your appointment request, this strategy keeps the door open, allows you to provide value and gives you permission to call the prospect back. Hopefully, during the next contact in a week or so, the prospect may be more receptive to your appointment request.

You may decide that, depending upon the circumstances, a two phone call approach is a better way to make many of your initial phone calls to certain prospects, such as business owners or more affluent individuals, and not just a way to salvage a rejection to an initial appointment request. This new way to make a phone call would be to introduce yourself, to inform them that you are not going to ask for an appointment but that you would like their permission to send an *Email Concept,* about an issue that may be of interest to them. After they have a few days to review it, you could suggest calling back to see if a casual lunch might be appropriate. Sound too radical, this two phone call approach? So did going from a one-interview sales approach to a two-interview sales approach in the 1970s.

Today's consumer is more skeptical than at any other time in history. Before the consumer feels comfortable developing a business relationship, one's trust needs to have been established. There is no better way to initiate a trust relationship than to provide value to a prospect before a contact is made. Providing the prospect with educational information is providing "value." It demonstrates, even from your initial contact, that your focus is on "giving" and not just "getting."

Email Concepts will differentiate you from the competition; certainly the *Email Concept* strategy will be unique and distinct. The *Email Concept* has an advantage over encouraging prospects to go to your Web site. You know when the prospect receives an *Email Concept* and you can be signaled when it has been opened. If the prospects are technologically proficient, the chance of them reviewing your material is greater than if it were a printed brochure. An *Email Concept* is more contemporary, distinct and controlled than directing a prospect to a Web site. If you don't have access to *Email Concepts* that you can forward to your prospects or clients, you are already getting behind. Check out: www.emailconcept.com. *Email Concepts*™ are available to anyone. Ask yourself; can I deliver what the client or prospect wants in the way that they want it? If not, you will eventually notice the consequences.

Technology is always evolving. It is no longer in opposition to relationship building. It is a relationship enhancer. You must keep current with how technology can provide better ways for communicating with your prospects. In the world of the new "Darwinian" technology, only the fastest will survive. Don't get left behind.

Here is a copy of an Email Concept™
on Excess Retirement Options

For Jack Prospect

Providing *Valuable* Information Of Particular Interest To You!

Compliments of
Joe Financial Advisor

Continue >>

You Are Being Discriminated Against!

The IRS has rigid limitations and penalties on how much business owners and highly paid executives can contribute into their personal accounts in their company's Qualified Retirement Plan.

What's the impact? | Continue >> |

You Won't Like This...

Almost ALL of your employees will receive substantially more proportionate income at retirement than you will...

Show me

| Continue >> |

A Widening Retirement Income Gap

*An unwanted surprise at retirement;
A serious future problem...YOURS!*

What do I do?

> **Continue >>**

Don't Be Uninformed

Don't find yourself saying...
"I was too busy to get the facts."

Will your reasons for **"not knowing"**
the facts make sense at retirement?

What is the solution? | Continue >> |

"Excess" Retirement Options

*Tired of being **tax penalized** because of your success? Want to **accumulate more** retirement money on a **tax advantaged** basis? Request information on "IRS allowable" Excess Retirement Options. Retirement gives NO second chances.*

Avoid the loss...Get the facts!

Click to exit	**Click to request sample plans**

"Excess" Retirement Options

Thank you for reviewing the Email Concept on "Excess" Retirement Plans. Please allow 48 hours if you requested sample plans.

CLOSE

What communication technology should I be utilizing to enhance my relationship with my prospects and clients. (i.e., newsletters, email concepts, etc)

Brochures – Necessary or Not?

Most local marketing in the financial services industry is poorly done. It has consisted primarily of distributing company and product brochures, a few local agents doing some occasional print advertisements and, in the last few years, a little training on target market identification. Why has marketing been so overlooked? Because, for years, marketing didn't have to be done. Selling and prospecting were the whole game...but no longer. Marketing must become your new business platform if you are going to survive. You must create an annual marketing plan that should be the lifeblood of your business, your yearly roadmap that directs all of your actions.

There are over one million financial advisors in the United States. Guess what? Most of them have the same brochures that you do. Only the covers are different. Your job in the new marketing environment is to create a brand personality that truly stands apart, is unique, distinct and differentiated from the competition. Marketing is *getting the consumer to notice you first!* It is achieved by doing things differently. It is not achieved by getting them to notice that you do what everyone else does, even if you can prove that you do it a little better.

Brochures can play a role in your image creation, but they are a very minor factor in building your brand personality. They are similar to supporting actors in a movie; not nearly as important as the lead actor, and the personality he or she brings to the screen. Don't develop your supporting actors' before getting your leading actors' "strategy and personality" in place.

Brochures should never be used as mass mailing pieces to prospects that have never heard of you. Remember the *Prospect Fishbowl?* Where is your individualized list of future prospects within your market segment? If you don't have that complete, developing one is the first priority! Do you want to make your first impact at your first face-to-face encounter with the prospect, or before then? How much better would your results be if one thousand prospects noticed you and created an attraction for you before they ever met you? Would your sales soar? Sure they would. People buy you, not product. People give interviews most easily to people they like. Your job is to create "likeability" for yourself and to create

> *Your job is to create "likeability"... We trust people whom we like.*

a constant familiarization. We trust people whom we like. It is the single greatest element that creates the strongest and most lasting perception.

So, where do brochures fit in? If you are going to have one, brochures need to be personalized to you instead of to your company. Most traditional brochures promote nothing distinct. They promote product and services. An effective brochure should promote your personal differentiation and likeability, not product. It should show your commonality to the prospect. It is only when you know your market segment as individuals that you can put together a personal brochure that talks about your specialty and how you personally relate to the market. Specialization elevates value perception. A narrower focus attracts greater appeal. The brochure that can visibly show your "likeability" and differentiation to a specific market segment can add credibility to your image.

How often have you gotten excited about a brochure you received from a financial company? Are yours just like those? Marketing is about creativity and innovation, not imitation. If you are going to use a brochure, have one created and make it personal. Reveal who you are, not just in business but also in real life. Make it distinctly different and unique from anything you have ever seen. Let it be a differentiator, not another imitation.

Write any ideas that you may have about creating a brochure that would have more specific and personal appeal to your identified market segment.

Producing a Radio Talk Show Program and Becoming a Local Celebrity

We have already discussed why traditional print advertising is the single greatest waste of money that most agents and financial advisors ever spend. Radio advertising is, also, at the top of that "waste of money" list. First of all, it is expensive. Therefore, it doesn't get done with much regularity, but even if it did, it rarely focuses on a cohesive market segment. Secondly, the station programming may focus on a specific age bracket of listeners, but this is hardly a criterion for market segmentation or individualization. However, radio is one area that may provide an exception to the rule for those who have the talent and desire to pursue this opportunity.

Radio is still a medium that can create local celebrity status in a very short period of time, if you have the ability and personality to communicate over the airwaves in a talk show format. We have helped financial advisors produce numerous radio talk shows that are still on the air today. These "everyday" advisors are now celebrities within their communities. Not a week passes without someone commenting to them about their radio talk shows. Listeners believe that these advisors are superior to others in their field. Even prospects who don't listen to the show but are given an audiotape (which cost less than one-dollar to produce, which includes the plastic case and insert cover) from the programs titled "The Ten Most Frequently Asked Financial Questions" as a promotional piece also believe that the advisors must be more advanced and therefore preferable to their competition.

These financial advisors have created consumer attraction and preference through radio talk shows. Financial radio talk shows are, and will continue to be, in high demand. The radio talk show celebrities can easily accumulate large *Prospect Fishbowls* of names by making a regularly sent financial newsletter available and encouraging the listeners to call a voice mail phone number or to contact their Web site to be put on the distribution list. Events can also easily be promoted and encouraging listeners to call in to request personal meetings will result in at least four to eight calls per week. Being a celebrity on a weekly or daily radio program creates an impact before the prospect has met you. This is marketing, not because of radio ads but because of the visibility, the uniqueness and the differentiation of YOU within the market place.

financial advisors... created consumer attraction and preference through radio talk shows

The audiotapes that you can have produced for one-dollar are far less expensive and are more effective than other alternatives in the industry. They are not self-promoting. They are recordings of actual questions and answers that help build a quality perception for the consumer and defines "why you". This is a far more convincing promotional piece for differentiating you than a generic brochure or a self-promotional audiotape.

There are two ways to produce an effective radio show. One is to find a local talk show station (usually an AM station) and explore its interest in having a financial call-in show. The show should last for one hour. Don't be surprised if they expand it to one and one-half hours in the near future. Talk time around commercials is approximately seventeen minutes during every thirty minutes of airtime. You can answer three questions per half-hour. You should broadcast during the weekday, not on weekends. Afternoon drive time starting around 3:00 p.m. is ideal. The local cellular telephone companies will assign a courtesy speed dial option (one number plus *) for drivers calling in during broadcast time if you will promote the cellular company and the number. You can announce this during the broadcast. It just adds more credibility to your new celebrity status.

Selling advertising spots produces the largest portion of a radio stations income and our financial shows were rated close, if not second, to Rush Limbaugh in popularity. Now, I will not comment on whether I am a Rush Limbaugh fan, but I did like the comparative ratings. The station made a lot of money by having a no-cost, popular show of this magnitude, which they could load with advertisements. Everyone was happy: the station, the advertisers, the listeners and the "celebrity" financial advisors. You should be able to convince the station to let you do the show for free for at least four to twelve

> *You should be able to convince the station to let you do the show for free...*

weeks while they measure its popularity. If they charge you a nominal fee, the agreement should be renegotiated to even less, or nothing, after the first quarter as the show becomes popular, and it will. Get a tape of a financial talk show from a radio program broadcast somewhere in the United States, give it to the station and discuss the benefits of producing a similar program. Financial programs are popular with listeners and both you and the station will be pleased with the results.

As you are getting established, you may have to ask friends, clients and business associates to call in questions for approximately three weeks. Make sure their questions are related to wealth, retirement and financial investment issues and not insurance. You can develop a list of good questions such as, "How do I best diversify my 401(k) plan at work and is it OK to put most of my contribution into my own company's stock? It has really been performing well and it is one of my options." You may need to have a "theme" to talk about for the first few weeks as the show gets off the ground. Make sure the theme is investment based and not insurance based. The public regards

> *They want to hear about "WEALTH, INVESTMENT, RETIREMENT and PROFIT" issues.*

insurance, even equity based variable life, as an expense. Disability income and long-term care insurance are also regarded as expenses. NO ONE wants more expenses and listeners are not interested in listening to a talk show program based on expense items. They want to hear about "WEALTH, INVESTMENT, RETIREMENT and PROFIT" issues.

It is unlikely that you will ever receive a call-in question about insurance. That should tell you something. Although you will have lots of opportunities to sell a lot of life and disability insurance in planning interviews with people who call-in to meet with you, it is not what you use to attract attention or to gather a listener-base over the airwaves. Very soon, you will have plenty of calls coming into your talk show and their questions will all be on investment issues. Talking about tax issues are also good if you get a lull in call-ins. Variable annuities are good subject matter, but be ready when someone calls to challenge you on the justification of the inside mortality and management expenses versus a mutual fund and the long-term taxable gain advantage. The more specific your answers are, the better your ratings will be and the more call-ins you will get.

The more specific your answers are, the better your ratings will be...

Your compliance department will need to be notified that you have a show. They are fully aware that there is nothing you can do to prepare or send in for their review. This does not mean that you have no responsibility to meet compliance standards when answering questions from your listeners. You definitely do. It should go without saying that you can't guarantee returns or make projections. Know the rules.

One of the greatest fears about being on radio is not knowing an answer to a question. You don't have to worry about not knowing an answer or having someone call to harass you. The radio station has a screener who answers the calls and then asks what the caller's question is. The screener will then type the question on a computer prompter screen in front of you so that you know who is on hold and to what the question pertains. You will probably want to have some research material and computer support with you. If you don't know the answer, instruct your screener to tell the caller that you have other people on hold, get the caller's number and ask to call him or her back personally. Once your show develops a following, you will have numerous callers backed up, holding with questions to be answered. Select the ones you know that you can handle the best and answer those on the air.

A great suggestion is to produce the show in partnership with another financial advisor in your firm. You may also want an administrative assistant present who can access research information on the computer for the next question while you are answering the current question. Our most popular shows had two financial advisor personalities. Don't bring in other professionals, very often, to share the show, such as attorneys or CPAs. Once in a month should be the limit. The show needs to promote YOU, not an outside attorney or CPA. Using two financial advisors does have one advantage in that you will quickly learn how to play off of each other. When one of you knows the answer better than the other, it is an easy hand-off to that person. Plus, you can make fun of each other and feel the audience laugh with you. Very quickly you will create "likeability"; "likeability" is the most important initial element for developing trust in a relationship.

Very quickly you will create "likeability"; "likeability" is the most important initial element for developing trust in a relationship.

Producing a Three-Minute Daily Broadcast Radio Show

Instead of doing a live talk show, consider producing a three-minute broadcast or vignette to be aired at the same time every day, Monday through Friday. The first one that I originally helped launch is still running today. It is called "Managing Money Based On God's Principles," a Christian financial show. Two financial professionals record two weeks' worth of vignettes (ten "three-minute" programs) every other week. This takes a maximum of ninety minutes and the radio station runs them at 7:45 a.m. every weekday. The recording is always done at the radio station, therefore, you incur no outside recording expense. Once you have accumulated sixty good vignettes, you can rotate the same material every three months. Make minor changes to the existing ones and record a few new ones when appropriate to keep the series contemporary. Because these are prerecorded spots, they do need to be sent to your compliance department for approval. Again, make sure that all the subjects are financial and investment related. You can test insurance-related topics for yourself. It will be quickly evident that the program produces no calls that day.

This show is broadcast on a fundamental Christian radio station and yields ten to eighteen call-ins per week. Within twelve months, the financial advisors created a *Prospect Fishbowl* of over one thousand call-in names by offering their free newsletter. This station has a cohesive group of listeners, who share a deep religious belief, which is an anomaly to most secular stations. As this truly was a cohesive market segment that could be individualized, the two advisors began and sponsored their first annual prayer breakfast, which brought in over two hundred people. The advisors' exposure through radio produced continual invitations to speak at local events. They became widely known in the Christian community as celebrities, and became actively involved in the city's Christian Business Expo and a number of other business and social opportunities, which were centered on their faith. Each quarter, they put together investment seminars based on biblical principles and announced them on radio. They also sent invitations to their *Prospect Fishbowl,* which now included the one thousand call-in names for

> ...the financial advisors created a Prospect Fishbowl of over one thousand call-in names by offering their free newsletter.

their newsletter. They put together an audiotape of their "Ten Most Requested Financial Topics," which they handed out enthusiastically. The audiotape proved to be significantly more meaningful than a simple business card when they met with new prospects and existing clients. They also used their audiotape as an "interest hook" when

They were having an impact on prospects before they met them...

requesting an initial appointment by offering to bring a free copy with them when they met the prospect... GET THE IDEA? They were becoming Identity Branded to a specific market segment. They were having an impact on prospects before they met them, rather than waiting until their first face-to-face encounter. They were *getting the prospect to notice them first* in a market segment where they themselves were emotionally committed. **This is marketing at its best!**

IDENTITY BRANDING

The following script is typical of their three-minute vignettes

Opening the broadcast – *the program's theme music is playing*

DJ Opens: *"It's time for our daily broadcast, "Managing Money Based On God's Principles," with your hosts Brad Smith and Kevin Hanner. If you have a financial question you would like answered, give us a call on our toll free number at 1-800-000-0000. Here are Brad and Kevin, professionals and registered representatives with (broker dealer) in (city) with today's question (or strategy).*

Brad: *(reads question or announces the theme) "We have a question from a listener today that reads, 'I have been in my company's 401(k) plan for a number of years now but don't know if I am investing in the right funds to get the best return. Everyone seems to have an opinion but isn't there some kind of practical formula or advice you can give us?' "*

Kevin: *"Many listeners have expressed to us their frustration with not knowing how their 401(k) works and how they can maximize their benefits from it."*

Brad: *"That is true. And a lot of times people who feel this way end up frustrated or too embarrassed to ask questions or, worse yet, they hold back on how much they contribute to their retirement plan."*

Kevin: *"You know, Brad, a recent Wall Street Journal article said that most people do not understand their 401(k) plan and that they end up investing poorly and then miss out on the biggest gains. It's not just an occasional occurrence. It happens all the time."*

Brad: *"Another one of our listeners about a month ago called from the city of Thomasville and expressed the same concern. The good news was that she was contributing to her 401(k) plan and had done well, but it wasn't diversified. She was just never really comfortable*

148

with not having any defined strategy...it made her nervous."

Kevin: *"I remember, Brad, she was mostly invested in her own company's stock with about twenty-five percent in another option. Although it had done well, her company's stock was trending down and the other option she had chosen didn't look promising for the next twelve months. As we spoke for a while, she realized that she had no investment strategy, no yearly rebalancing strategy and very little diversification."*

Brad: *"You know, Kevin, we provided information that helped her create a professional investment strategy that was more appropriate for her age and guided her into diversifying her account among four investment options within her plan. Now she doesn't have to worry about the account every day and she knows how to rebalance her account every twelve months for safety and to hopefully get the best return."*

Kevin: *"You know, Brad, in the Bible, God talks a lot about the importance of gaining wisdom and understanding. In Proverbs 4:6 it says, 'Do not forsake wisdom and she will protect you.' I think that applies to all areas of our lives."*

Brad: *"You're right, Kevin. Listeners...don't ignore your 401(k) plan or try to guess at how you should be investing. Your mistakes could cost you the retirement that you have dreamed about. If you would like an information packet on the best strategies for investing in your 401(k) plan, please call us at 1-800-000-0000. Don't delay. The information packet is FREE...just call."*

DJ closes: *(theme music starts to play) "If you would like the information packet on today's topic or if you have a question related to finances or money, please call our number at 1-800-000-0000. And be sure to join Brad and Kevin tomorrow morning here at (station) for the daily broadcast of 'Managing Money Based on God's Principles.'"*

This script is an example of a one-minute secular broadcast

Opening the broadcast – *Theme music playing from the song "MONEY"*

DJ opens: *"Your future financial success is a matter of money and strategy. So with answers to your daily questions, here is (name), your professional here in (city), registered representative with (XXXXXXXXXXX) and host of your 7:45 a.m. daily broadcast, 'The One-Minute Financial Strategy.' "*

Financial professional (YOU!): *"Retirement planning is a critical issue for women. Did you know that, according to the National Center for Women and Retirement Research, 85% of all women will die alone either because of being widowed, divorced, or never having married."*

"73% of retired women have no retirement plan and the AARP reports that of the 12% of all elderly people living in poverty, 74% of them are women."

"If you're a woman, you have an 80%-90% chance that someday you will be solely responsible for your own finances. You can't afford to be uninformed about investing and finances."

"If you would like our FREE booklet entitled 'Empowering Financial Information for Women,' call us at _____. Again that number is _____."

DJ closes: *(theme music starts playing) "Don't delay. Requesting additional information is free. Our daily financial broadcast may last only one minute, but your future will last a lifetime. That phone number for the free information is _____."*

"Managing Money Based on God's Principles"

The New **94.1** WWGL

"Today's Best Christian Music"

**Kevin Hanner & Brad Smith
can be heard each morning
at 7:45 am on WWGL and
can be contacted at (336) 852-8650.**

"The plans of the diligent lead to profit."
Proverbs 5:5

"Creating Simple and Unique Solutions to Complex Issues"

"Your Money Matters"

600 WSJS

John Hardy and Gib McEachran can be heard
every Wednesday from 3:30 to 5:00 pm on WSJS
and contacted daily at (336) 852-8650

"Every man is the architect of his own fortune."
- Sallust

152

If producing a radio program has created an interest, write down the station that comes to your mind, the type of program (talk or prerecorded) that appeals to you and any other issues that may apply. Just write down your thoughts and see what happens.

Build A Well-Structured Branding Plan

If you are an agency manager, it is neither necessary nor practical to focus your entire agency on a single targeted group. Much like a law firm, however, you do need to help each associate find a unique focus in which they can become deeply and emotionally involved. Help them to individually construct a well-structured branding and marketing plan and then commit to managing it with them. Guy Kawasaki, author of *Selling the Dream,* says, "The obvious benefit of a plan is that it serves as the guiding light...In addition, writing a plan forces you to think critically, to better understand your cause, and to communicate with others in the organization." The more complete the plan, the better your communication will be and the better the support you can extend, particularly to your more established sales professionals.

If your sales associates are not willing to go out of their way to get involved with the market segment(s) that they are considering as a focus, this group is not for them. If they want to defend their marketing problems solely as either product or advanced knowledge needs, start looking for their replacements. Regardless of their seniority or their past success, they won't reach their full potential in this new environment, unless they have a marketing plan. Without a marketing plan, the chances are they won't even survive.

Working harder...will not substitute as a solution to market access problems.

Working harder will eventually not overcome the loss in income that a worsening market-access problem will incur. Being coached to get better organized, to become more efficient and to become a better delegator, though all worthy goals, will not substitute as a solution to market-access problems. You must meet the new marketing expectations of the consumer in order to survive. You must become a "package of value," that is far more significant than the product sold or the promise to provide good service. Dr. Thomas Stanley, in *Networking With the Affluent,* sums it up thusly, "Sales and marketing professionals focusing on their own needs, their own products, their own services, their own fees and commissions, and not on those of their targets, will not be successful in this arena." Regarding the needs of your target markets, they must be able to describe your differentiation, distinction and uniqueness relative to the competition. They must be able to answer the question, *"Why you?"* Answering that question by creating consumer preference and "mindshare" in an individualized market can only be accomplished from becoming...

DISTINCT, and if not...EXTINCT!

IDENTITY BRANDING

How to Get Started

Becoming Unique and Distinct

Building an Identity Brand is more than a strategic planning process; it's an active relationship process. Regis McKenna, author of *Real Time,* says, "Brand is an active experience." It therefore requires a structured plan for consistent review as to progress and accountability to your strategy. You must create a perception of

> *Building an Identity Brand is...an active relationship process...*

uniqueness relative to the competition. The prospect is incapable of judging expertise, service promises or even product superiority, but they can judge whether they are attracted to your brand personality. You can't do the same things as the competition and expect to increase prospect attraction. Neither should you focus on taking away a portion of market share from your competitor. You must focus on owning the entire market segment. You must create a solid basis of differentiation that captures prospect "mindshare," makes constant impressions and creates a distinctive perception that you offer a higher quality "package of value." By becoming unique and distinct, you will be the recipient of many benefits.

The Six Benefits of Identity Branding YOU

James R. Gregory and Jack G. Wiechmann, authors of *Marketing Corporate Image,* say, "Branding is a declaration of who we are, what we believe and why you should put your faith in [us] our company." In today's market, the expanding breadth of products, everyone's claims of superiority and the intrusive marketing methods used in an attempt to sell them, bewilder the consumer. Roman G. Hiebing Jr. and Scott W. Cooper, authors of *The One-Day Marketing Plan,* say,

"...the consumer does not have the time or energy to know everything necessary to make the right choice." They are frustrated in today's advertising and product proliferation environment. There is simply too much product noise in the market place. Consumers want to simplify their life choices. They are becoming far more concerned with making a decision on "whom to believe" than they are in determining "what to believe." That is why branding has become such a focus for tangible products. Once the brand is in the consumer's mind, everything else becomes much less of a concern. Branding YOU as the product of choice brings with it the same benefit as branding a tangible product. These are the six specific benefits you can expect:

1. Easier and perpetual access to prospects

2. Faster acceptance by new prospects referred to you in complementary markets

3. Shortened sales cycle

4. Larger average sales

5. Maintaining a defined focus is easier

6. Stronger loyalty within your organization

You will see...perpetual access open up to your prospects...a prospect highway.

Once you have completed the decision as to the market(s) segment toward which you are going to focus and direct your branding efforts, you will begin to see an almost immediate improvement in market access to your prospects. You will see an easier and a perpetual access open up to your prospects, what I refer to as the benefit of building a prospect highway. It can be argued as to whether the change is internal (psychological) or external but, regardless of the nature of the change, it is real. You will begin to view your market with ownership. You will begin to think in terms of "giving" and not "getting." It is now YOUR valuable asset whose future growth is in your hands. Once you begin to implement your branding plan of "familiarity and distinction," you will begin to see the market access door open to your requests to introduce your services to the new prospect.

As your career continues to develop, you will always have opportunities for expanding or refocusing your market in line with your skill level. The biggest mistake that most sales professionals make is working with people who are below their skill level. Once you have determined your ideal profile of a prospect, don't violate it. Remember the days when you scraped, clawed and fought your way to any sale that you could get your hands on? Don't you wish now that you would have focused your efforts more? Think of all the time you wasted on all of those prospects who looked so promising but never worked out. Well, don't regress. It's easy, but detrimental, to find yourself chasing a sale that you have no business pursuing. Guy E. Baker, CLU, MSFS, one of the leading producers in the insurance industry and *Top of the Table* since 1977, says in his book *Why People Buy,* "I still find it hard to say 'no' to a potential prospect. I have had to discipline myself to only focus on the 'profile' prospects. I want to talk to people who are going to enhance my long-term business objectives. If there is no rational reason to accept a case that is outside my business plan, then I need to walk away."

As your market reputation develops, your existing market segment will provide opportunities for you to be introduced to new markets and prospects that fit your prospect profile equally as well. If you have positioned yourself effectively in your initial market segment, you will have faster market acceptance to these new prospects because of your reputation and the "lead in" that you will naturally receive. Once your branding plan is structured, you will find it easy to expand to include these new prospects and to make a similar impact on them as you have on your initial market segment.

The selling sales cycle within your market segment will also become more efficient the greater your Identity Brand becomes. You will also see your average sales size increase. This would not have happened if you had maintained your efforts solely on finding referrals and had resisted getting involved in a structured marketing plan. The industry has always promoted two skills. The *selling skill* was what was needed to convince a prospect to part with his money for your product. It was the "getting skill." The *prospecting skill* was learning to identify a prospect who had a need you could meet and the ability to pay for it. Now you need a third skill, the *MARKETING SKILL,* which is different from the prospecting skill.

> *The selling sales cycle...*
> *will become more efficient*

Remember, the marketing skill is learning how to capture "mindshare" before a contact is made. It is different than the prospecting skill. It is all about how to create an Identity Brand where trust becomes established before the contact has been initiated. This is the skill that allows producers to SOAR. It is the skill that makes the competition go away and look elsewhere for a prospect. It is the skill that allows you to claim ownership to a market segment that eventually even the competition must acknowledge is owned by you. Regis McKenna, author of *Relationship Marketing,* writes, "...winning over the customer's mind is the central challenge of marketing." Guy E. Baker, CLU, MSFS in his book *Why People Buy,* says, "Successful marketing occurs when

> *Regis McKenna, author*
> *of Relationship Marketing,*
> *"...winning over the*
> *customer's mind is the*
> *central challenge of*
> *marketing."*

you are on your client's shelf." (referring to the "shelf of your mind").
He goes on to say, "You have succeeded when you are front and center
and he thinks of you every time the products and services you
represent are mentioned." What can you do to position yourself on
the "shelf" of your client's mind? That is what marketing is all about.
That is why Guy Baker is one of the top twenty producers in the
United States. He understands and works at marketing, not just
selling and prospecting.

Maintaining your defined focus becomes much easier once you have
your Identity Branding plan formulated. It is all too easy to get
trapped into working with the prospect with whom you never should
have gotten involved. That
continues to occur to those
who have only developed
selling and prospecting skills
and have overlooked marketing.
Guy E. Baker, CLU, MSFS
says, "What a nice situation to
be in, to have a list of prequalified prospects who know
what you do, who want to talk
to you, and who are accessible
because of your marketing
skills." When you have your market segment individualized, you have
a much easier time maintaining your focus. If your intended market
were simply identified as "small business owners," would there not
be some small business owners with whom you shouldn't work
because they are too small or unprofitable? Does every small
business owner fit your profile? Even if they did, how can you get
on "the shelf of their minds" if you can't individualize them? How
can you create "mindshare"? You can't! You must individualize your
market to create "mindshare" and to maintain focus on your defined
prospect profile.

> *Guy E. Baker, CLU, MSFS says, "What a nice situation to be in, to have a list of pre-qualified prospects who know what you do, who want to talk to you, and who are accessible because of your marketing skills."*

The final benefit is the strong loyalty you will create within your organization. If you are a sales professional who has support staff, these employees will take on more responsibility and involvement in helping you become Identity Branded than they ever did to help promote your company. Your company is an impersonal object that creates product. Your support staff always saw you as the business, but this may be the first time that they clearly see the objective, to promote you as the local brand. They will now see you as the company and they realize that their promotional efforts will reflect not only on your reputation, but also on their prestige within the community. They see this objective as becoming a part of something greater than a "sale professional's staff." They become part of a *local market brand.*

If you are a manager of an agency, you have an opportunity to utilize your ability to help your sales professionals market their own identity. This creates local identity and differentiation for your agency and becomes your distinction as compared to the competition. This is your advantage. It is not the difference in your company's products as compared to the competition that attracts new hires. The new recruit and administration support people that you hope to hire view all companies as essentially the same. When they see the agency as distinctive, their interest increases. Once hired, they will display pride and loyalty in an agency that is unique. If you want to hire the best people, become known as the best in helping sales professionals become Identity Branded. From this perspective, you will become the most attractive company for which to work.

There are five basic ingredients in Identity Branding. Each step will require some serious thought, but the benefits far outweigh the effort involved.

Five Basic Ingredients For Establishing An Identity Brand

1. **Individualize your market** and determine to "own" it. Regis McKenna, author of *Relationship Marketing,* says, "When you own the market...you define the standards in that market."

2. **Create a yearly structured branding business plan** that specifies progress review dates at least four times per year. Your structured plan should include all the elements of the diagram shown below.

3. **Create plan components** that the client and prospect regards as high-value, memorable, creative and differentiated from the competition. Lynn Upshaw, author of *Building Brand Identity,* says, "A brand's positioning establishes its credibility, but its likeability is a direct function of its personality." Frequently give them something to like that has substance.

4. **Consistent Familiarity** - These two words are critical to the success of your plan and its impact on the prospect. You must provide *consistent familiarity* to your audience.

5. **Patience and Persistence** - Give your plan at least one year before critiquing the impact. You will be pleased. Don't stop prematurely or "water down" your plan during the year. The greatest mistakes most agents make are giving up prematurely and not following through.

Your job is to create an Identity Brand that creates a visible distinction, a competitive advantage and answers the question, "Why You?" Once you have accomplished that goal, you will never again have a prospecting problem.

Your job is to create an Identity Brand that...answers the question, "Why You?"

IDENTITY BRANDING MODEL

The Adventurous Future

You are about to embark on the most exciting challenge you will ever confront. The marketing revolution that is going to grip America will be the stuff from which generational stories are made. It will be like sitting on your great-great-great-grandfather's lap and hearing about the first airplane that he ever saw fly overhead. It will be like seeing the first broadcast TV show or like being present to see a TV show broadcast in color for the first time. However, this change is not about a new revolutionary product being developed and introduced to the public. This change is not just about consumers wanting more information, wanting to be treated more professionally or wanting to know more about the reasoning behind your recommendations. This change is about the consumer having more alternatives than ever before for purchasing anything and everything they may want. It is about the consumer being in control of directing the selling process. It is about the total reversal of how goods are sold, distributed and accessed. The challenge requires a response to meeting the client's demands for what they want, when they want it, where they want it and how they want it.

You have an opportunity to not only survive this change but to prosper from it. Survival is dependent upon your ability to adopt and adapt. Those who delay the process will fail. Speed is critical. You will learn by doing, not by cautiously plotting and planning. You will learn by making mistakes. The greatest determining factor necessary for success will be how fast you can recognize your mistakes and recover from them. Resiliency will be key. Quick decisions, coupled with resiliency when errors are made, will be far superior to good decisions that are implemented six months too late.

> *Survival is dependent upon your ability to adopt and adapt.*

Lynn Upshaw, author of *Building Brand Identity,* says, "Interactive communications are here, not in their ultimate form and only a fraction of their ultimate size, but their existence is undeniable, and their future is assured." He goes on to say, "...interactive media offers an advanced form of...relationship marketing" but "Still, there is a real question about how many of today's successful marketers will be able to make the turn into a contemporized selling environment." Interactive communications will play an important role in this marketing revolution and coupling them with building an Identity Brand will be imperative for your business to flourish.

Your effectiveness in getting a sale by demonstrating that your product and service are superior to the competition has diminished, if not totally vanished. A brand is much more than product today. The product you sell is no longer any more singularly defined than McDonald's® defining hamburgers as their business. If McDonald's had defined their business as hamburgers, they would have failed. If they were in hamburger competition, they would come out last. McDonald's attraction is built from the same base that your future needs to be built from, the formulation of a distinct personality, a Brand created and maintained through experiences.

The newly empowered consumers no longer want to listen to the typical sales approach. Just "getting in" to see them is harder. The average person is so squeezed for time today that their tolerance level is as low as it has ever been. They are more hurried, less patient and less tolerant than at any time in history, and it won't

the more distinct your Identity Brand, the greater your chances for success.

get better. The sales professional's survival will be dependent on creating an emotional connection with prospects, before engaging them in even the initial conversation. The "trust sale" will need to have been made before they have met you. The bottom line: the more distinct your Identity Brand, the greater your chances for success.

This next marketing revolution will embrace the new communication technology to maximize the new marketing skills. The two, marketing and technology are no longer adversaries. They are complementary. Both will be key to your future success.

The traffic on this new marketing road is picking up speed. It may appear to be subtle now, but that is about to change. You cannot afford to be lingering on the roadside or yielding to the other traffic. You cannot patiently wait on the ramp for just the right time to enter this new marketing super highway. Yielding to the other traffic will be tantamount to the yield sign reading, "Stop – Give Up All Hope." If you don't pick up speed, you will become a fatality. Determine that this new journey is going to be fun and get into the fast lane. The destination will be better than any other that you have ever witnessed, but the trip is a one-time offering. It is only for those who want to go NOW.

See you there!

IDENTITY BRANDING

IDENTITY BRANDING

Keeping On Track

Summary

The approaches in this book are far from exhaustive in giving ways to become unique, distinct and Identity Branded within your local market. However, they point the way to the sort of activities that are required if you are to succeed in the new consumer environment. The challenge for future success does not lie in the traditional selling and prospecting skills of yesterday, nor in the product development department's belief that the "Best" product always rises to the top. Rather, future success lies in the hands of those who focus on marketing, implement meaningful strategies and ultimately answer the consumer's question, "Why you?" before ever meeting them.

Your new focus on marketing won't come naturally, but your successful results will be significant and personally fulfilling. It will be easy to regress, but the consequence of not adapting will eventually prove fatal. It will take effort and concentration to remember that marketing is not about trying to get the sales professional to maintain a positive attitude; it is not about proclaiming a general market definition (i.e., small business market) as your marketing focus and believing that suffices for a marketing plan; it is not about identifying a list of prospect names to target sell; it's not about learning how to close more effectively and it is not about acquiring more advanced training; it's not about print advertising or creating better looking brochures; it's not about service, wave-mailings, direct-mail solicitations, telemarketing, Web sites, or trying to do the same things that the competition is doing, but proclaiming that you do them better. *It's about having a known system for identifying your prospect community by individual names and then branding your distinct, unique, intriguing and differentiated Identity Brand into their minds.*

Most companies expect the sales professional to complete technical, continuing education credits each year to stay current. They should also expect them to complete on-going training for marketing development. The offices and companies that stay current in marketing, partner in developing local marketing plans and consistently manage and monitor their progress, will retain their people, increase their sales, recruit the new talent that they pursue, increase their profits and have a strategic competitive advantage over the competition.

The letter on the next page, "A Mid-Year Review for Sales Professionals," and the forms that follow may help you self-monitor your own progress as you learn and develop the new skills that the consumer is demanding. Don't get sidetracked. Don't allow marketing to be a secondary focus. Marketing is critical to your future success. Plan your strategy and maintain your persistency. If your strategy is "sound," success will follow.

A Mid-Year Review for Sales Professionals

Dear Sales Professional,

If you have read this book and the majority of your income is determined each year by incentive or commissions, I would encourage you to take a few minutes to read this letter and actively participate when it directs you to highlight or write your comments. This letter is your mid-year "challenge" letter. As a matter of fact, grab a hi-liter NOW and get ready to mark the areas that speak to you personally. This should allow for a self-critique of your understanding and proficiency of the many components within this book and allow you to self-evaluate your potential as compared to your performance so far this year. So, get your hi-liter (I am serious!) and read for about 2 minutes. (GET YOUR HI-LITER OUT NOW instead of deciding after you read that you should have listened and now need to read it again. Got it? OK, now have fun, highlight anything that directly affects you ...let's go!)

The first challenge is to be reflective and honest with yourself about your yearly results so far. ARE YOU SATISFIED? Use your hi-liter and mark either YES or NO right here. (Did you do it?) We will come back to this question later. (Yes, you can circle one of the answers if you have a pen instead of a hi-liter). Next, write in a percentage for each of the three areas listed below, indicating what area was most responsible for impeding your desired results. (If you are 100% satisfied with any one area, just leave it blank. If there were no product knowledge deficiencies that limited your results, that number would be a 0%. If you just didn't get around to seeing enough people and that was the only deficiency, Inadequate Prospect/Contact Activity would be 100% and be the only item marked. Your percentages cannot add up to more than 100%.)

- Inadequate Sales or Product Knowledge _____%
- Inadequate Focus on In-Office Tasks _____%
- Inadequate Prospect/Contact Activity _____%

If you are one-hundred percent satisfied with your progress this year, GREAT! But keep reading; you may still get a good idea.

Now, write in a "performance goal" based on income or prospect contacts that you should attain every month or quarter. This performance goal should be monetary if you are commissioned or on an incentive income program. It may also be a monthly contact goal if you are proactively responsible for personally meeting new prospects.

Goal: _____ per _____ (month or quarter).

Before we go any further with evaluations, take a minute to write down three personal "wants" that you hope to attain in the next twelve months. Remember these are personal wants. Do your best to stay away from items like your company production club or an incentive trip qualification. Make sure that these are material things that cost money, i.e., a new car, new furniture, a two-week vacation, a debt paid off, an amount of money saved or invested by years end. If it's a three-year monetary goal (i.e., saving $50,000 for down payment on a vacation home down payment), just list an amount that is attainable and measurable for the next twelve months. If it's a family cruise for next spring, how much will you save this year or each quarter? While you are listing your three items, imagine really wanting them. Try to feel the emotions you will experience and disappointment that others may have if you don't attain the goal that is needed to meet these "wants." Do you really want to do without? Circle the one most important "want" item, one that you will commit to attaining, and share this with the person in your life who is the most important to you.

	Item	Method for measuring progress
1)	_____	_____
2)	_____	_____
3)	_____	_____

(Remember to circle your most important item, the one that you will share!)

Now let's review some BUSINESS ELEMENTS that you should incorporate in order to meet your goals.

1) Do you have a **definite,** scheduled MID-WEEK CHECK-POINT for the one or two priority *activities* that you must accomplish in order to meet your financial goals? Write down when this occurs, or should occur, and specify what activity you are measuring. When is your mid-week checkpoint?

_____
_____

What and "how many" of whatever are you measuring?

_____
_____

2) What is the market segment(s) around which you want to build your business? How many individualized names can you gather from each segment? How will you begin creating a familiarization strategy? What ways can you think of to begin effectively networking within this market segment? Write down the names of your market segments:

_____
_____

What is the number of potential names within each segment:

_____

_____

How will you begin your *familiarization strategy* in each segment?

_____

_____

3) How many new names of prospects do you gather each week, month or quarter to add to your *Prospect Fishbowl?* If you don't constantly measure this, eventually you will find yourself working with prospects that don't fit your prospect profile and are below your skill level. You will find yourself wearing out your existing client base, prematurely trying to derive revenue from them and frustrating yourself with your attempts. How many new prospect names will you add?   #_____ per _____

How many total names will you have in your *Prospect Fishbowl* in the next six months? _____ 12 months? _____

4) How do you consistently familiarize yourself to your *Prospect Fishbowl?* Newsletters? Events? How do you appear distinct and differentiated from the competition? How are you creating an attraction that identifies you as the "brand of choice" within your market segment? Be specific:

_____

_____

5) What do you need to do to build an alliance with a complementary organization? Who will it be? What should be your first step? When will you take it?

_____

_____

6) What do you need to do to merge communication technology with relationship building? How are you building your email database? What technology plans are you pursuing in order to communicate with your clients and prospects in the future so that you meet their expectations? In what areas do you need to get more information? What is a reasonable deadline for implementation?

_____

_____

7) Determine to make an appointment every week, every two weeks or monthly with a new prospect, whose level of sophistication requires a joint-work effort with a more experienced associate or a specialist in your office. Determine to work "over your head" on a predetermined scheduled basis. You will increase your ability by leaps and bounds. Even if you ARE the experienced associate, let someone else carry the case that is beyond your skill level while you watch. Set a schedule for just one joint-work effort on a regular basis and honor it! Write down how often you will do this and what kind of reminder you will give yourself so that it doesn't get forgotten.

_____

_____

8) Commit to completing a *courageous* act every day before 10:00 a.m. A *courageous* act might be making that call to someone by whom you are intimidated. Maybe it is calling on a business owner for an appointment or contacting someone that you know from civic club but have never called on. The item changes every day and week, but a courageous act must always be a revenue producing activity. Signing up for a proficiency exam or approaching your boss about a raise does not qualify. A *courageous act* is about doing "scary" things that are easy to put off and always seem worse before you face them than after they are completed. No one becomes successful without tackling "scary" issues. The better you are, the more successful you become. And remember, do one act

by 10:00 a.m. each day. How will you track your *"cou*
Make a special place each day in your day timer?

Write your strategy. _____

_____

_____

9. Develop a habit of recording those items that you would consider
    VICTORIES at the end of each week. Maybe it was calling on a
    prospect that you had feared and it successfully resulted in an
    appointment. Maybe it was setting up a referral or endorsement
    luncheon that ended up quite successful. Maybe it was deciding
    to close a case with a client who had been stalling, for no apparent
    reason, and your efforts paid off. If you have young children,
    consider doing this as a family project with your kids. Establish a
    consistent time with your family, maybe at a meal or at bedtime
    on Friday night after the week is over. Label a small notebook
    "MY VICTORY LOG" and record your *victories*. You won't believe
    the increase in confidence this new reality will provide. It will
    become your children's favorite book...and yours. You are
    building new levels of confidence and pride. It is not based on
    hype. It is who you are. It is based on all the *victories* that we so
    easily forget; the *victories* we allow to become overshadowed by
    even the smallest setbacks. It's recognizing and giving yourself
    credit for the reality of how good you are. It is the main element
    for building self-esteem. Imagine the impact this would have on
    your children. How will you implement this?

    _____

    _____

Ok, this concludes your year-to-date challenge and self-evaluation.
The ideas that you have written down will help to propel your future
success. The future is going to be different and to succeed, you, too,
will have to change. Old methods and strategies will no longer work.
Even working harder will not suffice this time. You will need to look

.nd be different from the competition. You will need to have a more directed focus. You will have to have a familiarization plan that identifies you to your market segment prospects before you call on them. You will need to make an impact, not at the time of your first meeting, but far in advance of it. You will need to become an effective entrepreneur who builds a business on a marketing model instead of on a selling model. For those who are successful, the future will be bright. Your success is dependent on becoming DISTINCT...and if you don't, you can expect to become EXTINCT. It's entirely up to you.

Best wishes for a bright future,

Robert E Krumroy
President
Identity Branding, Inc.

Ten Challenge Questions
for Refocusing To A Market Segment

> "Never get so involved in your work that you neglect to keep those important marketing and public relations activities going. Your target market needs to hear from you regularly in your public relationship and marketing activities." William J. Bond, *Going Solo,* (NY, NY: McGraw-Hill, 1997)

1) What privileged service do my *A clients (top 20%)* receive?

_____

_____

What should I add?

_____

_____

2) How do my *A clients* know that they are a select class? What special event / function / service do I provide for them?

_____

_____

3) What do I expect from my *A clients* in return for what I extend to them?

_____

_____

How have I related this expectation to them?

_____

_____

4) How do I avoid personal involvement in my *B client* and *C client* service needs, yet make sure that those needs are being met (i.e., customer service rep, etc.)?

_____

_____

5) What market segment(s) of prospects (not clients) do I consistently communicate with using a specific strategy plan?

_____

_____

What *should* I, and *will* I do?

_____

_____

6) What unique and differentiated activities am I offering to my market segment(s) now to create an emotional connection?

_____

_____

7) What specific marketing activities will I conduct in the next twelve months to place me in front of significant groups of prospects within my market segment(s)?

_____

_____

How many unique marketing events will I conduct?

_____

8) How many prospects, that meet my prospect profile, will I add to my Prospect Fishbowl this year? _____

What will my total number be at year-end? _____

9) What consistent familiarization method will I use to capture "mindshare" of my clients and prospects within my *Prospect Fishbowl* (Be specific: e.g.,newsletters)?

_____

_____

How often? _____

10) What new things should I be doing that will make the greatest positive impact to my reputation and my accessibility to my market segment(s), in the next 5 years?

_____

_____

Methods for Cultivating Your "A" Clientele

1) Tell them, often, that they are special and appreciated.

2) Send flowers or birthday cakes (delivered personally to your top 20% on their birthdays). What will I do?

_____

_____

3) Have an appreciation event. What will I do?

_____

_____

4) Meet with every *A client* at least 2 times per year. How will I do this?

_____

_____

5) Get to know every *A client* on an individual basis. How will I do this?

_____

_____

6) Send a regular newsletter and include a handwritten note 8 times per year.

_____

_____

Comments:

_____

_____

7) Give extra service to your top 25-40 clients each year.

_____

_____

Ideas:_____

_____

8) Be punctual. Do what you promise.

References and Acknowledgements

1) Baker, Guy E. *(Why People Buy)* (Standel Publishing, 1995)
2) Baron, Gerald R. *(Friendship Marketing)* (Grants Pass, Oregon: The Oasis Press, 1997)
3) Beckwith, Harry *(Selling The Invisible)* (New York, NY: Warner Books, Inc., 1997)
4) Bond, William J. *(Going Solo)* (New York, NY: McGraw-Hill, 1997)
5) Boylan, Michael *(The Power To Get In)* (New York, NY: St. Martin's Press, 1997)
6) Clancey, Kevin J. and Robert S. Shulman *(Marketing Myths That are Killing Business)* (New York, NY: McGraw-Hill, 1995)
7) Conlon, Ginger, "No Turning Back," Sales and Marketing Management, December 1999, PP. 50-52, 54, 55.
8) Dale, Wally *(Collaborative Database Marketing)* (Washington, DC: GAMA Foundation, 1999)
9) Debelak, Don *(Marketing Magic)* (Adams Media Corp; 1997)
10) Gregory, James R. and Jack G. Wiechmann *(Marketing Corporate Image)* (Chicago: NTC Business Books, 1999)
11) Harding, Ford *(Creating Rainmakers)* (Holbrook, MA: Adams Media Corporation, 1998)
12) Hiebing Jr., Roman and Scott W. Cooper *(The One-Day Marketing Plan)* (Chicago: NTC Publishing Group, 1999)
13) Ingari, Frank "The Internet as a Marketing Medium," Strategy and Business, Fourth Quarter 1999, PP. 6-8.
14) Kawasaki, Guy *(Selling The Dream)* (New York, NY: Harper Collins Publishers, 1991)
15) Kennedy, Dan *(The Ultimate Marketing Plan)* (Holbrook, MA: Adams Media Corporation, 1991)
16) Lenzner, Robert and Ashlea Ebeling "A Wealth of Names – David Rockefeller Sr. is The Ultimate Rainmaker," Forbes, January 10, 2000, PP. 70, 71.
17) Levitt, Theodore *(The Marketing Imagination)* (New York, NY: The Free Press, 1986)
18) McKenna, Regis *(Real Time)* (Harvard Business School Press, 1999)
19) McKenna, Regis *(Relationship Marketing)* (Reading, MA: Addison-Wesley, 1998)
20) Misner, Ph. D., Ivan and Virginia Divine *(The Worlds Best Known Marketing Secret)* (Austin, Texas: Bard Press, 1999)
21) Palmer, Parker *(Let Your Life Speak)* (San Francisco, California: Jossey-Bass publishers, 2000)
22) Pritchett, Price *(New Work Habits For a Radically Changing World)* (Dallas, Texas: Pritchett & Associates, Incorporated, 1998)
23) Prince, Russ and Karen File *(Marketing Through Advisors)* (Cincinnati, Ohio: National Underwriter, 1996)
24) Ries, Al and Jack Trout *(Positioning – The Battle For Your Mind)* (New York, NY: Warner Books and McGraw-Hill, 1986)
25) Schmitt, Bernd H. *(Experiential Marketing)* (Free Press, 1999)
26) Stanley, Dr. Thomas *(Networking With The Affluent)* (New York, NY: McGraw-Hill, 1993)
27) Sullivan, Dan *(The 21st Century Agent)* (Toronto, Canada: The Strategic Coach Inc., 1995)
28) Upshaw, Lynn *(Building Brand Identity)* (John Wiley & Sons, Inc., 1995)

About the Author

Robert E. Krumroy, CLU, ChFC, is president of Identity Branding, Inc., an organization devoted to assisting the financial sales professional in creating a distinct and unique local market presence; a perception of *superior value*, that opens a prospect highway to a prospect community that welcomes their presence, creates a competitive advantage and solves the issue of "market access." Krumroy began his career as an insurance agent, transitioned into management and was recognized nationally as a sixteen-time National Management qualifier and one of the very few national Master-Agency Award qualifiers in the financial services industry. He is a featured columnist, a frequent article contributor to magazines, has served on the GAMA teaching faculty for "Best Practices" and is a highly sought after speaker. He has been introduced on many occasions as the most brilliant marketing mind in the financial services industry and has been a main platform presenter at most of the industry conventions.

As a Branding/Marketing consultant, author, columnist, speaker and "Branding Clinic" leader, he provides a wide range of resources for business, educational organizations and individuals including:

- Keynote Presentations
- Identity Branding Clinics (half-days)
- Comprehensive "Identity Branding Business Plan" Manuals and Workshops
- Strategic Identity Branding Consulting for National Companies
- Strategic Identity Branding Consulting for Local Offices
- Two Branding Newsletters for Sales Professionals to Send to Their Prospects and Clients: *Money Impact* and *Business Impact*
- Email Concepts™
- Market Segment Questionnaires, Evaluation and Identity Branding Penetration Planning Forms.
- *Free* Identity Branding Tip Email Every Six Weeks (Just sign up on the Web site)

For more information on the wide range of resources available from Robert Krumroy, visit our web site at:

www.identitybranding.com

or just call, email, write or fax:

Identity Branding, Inc.
2007 Yanceyville Street, Suite 270
Greensboro, NC 27405

Toll free: 1-800-851-8169
Fax: 1-336-303-7318
Email: Bob@identitybranding.com

To Order Books

Please mail, fax, or email your order on our Web site:

_____ copies at $16.95 each =_____
($16.95 U.S. currency; $22.95 in Canada)

Plus $3.00 shipping/handling =_____
(U.S. currency; $5.00 in Canada)

Total enclosed = _____

Please send book(s) to:

Name _____

Address _____

City_____State_____Zip_____

_____Visa _____Mastercard

Credit card number _____

Expiration date _____Phone # _____

Card holder's signature _____

Order on web site or by sending credit card, check, or money order to:

Identity Branding
2007 Yanceyville Street, Suite 270
Greensboro, NC 27405

1-800-851-8169
Fax: 336-303-7318; E-mail: info@identitybranding.com
Visit our website at: www.identitybranding.com